A PRACTICAL GUIDE TO
CREATIVE ACCOUNTING

A PRACTICAL GUIDE TO
CREATIVE
ACCOUNTING

Michael Jameson

KOGAN
PAGE

Copyright © Michael Jameson 1988

First published in Great Britain
in 1988 by Kogan Page Limited,
120 Pentonville Road, London N1 9JN

Reprinted 1988

British Library Cataloguing in Publication Data
Jameson, Michael
  A practical guide to creative accounting.
  1. Accounting
  I. Title
  657   HF 5637

  ISBN 1-85091-301-3 Hbk
  ISBN 1-85091-661-X Pbk

Printed and bound in Great Britain by
Biddles Limited, Guildford

Contents

1. **Accounting and Creative Accounting**   7
Introduction 7; Financial statements 9; The objectives
of accounting 15; The limitations of accounting 15;
The rules 17; What is creative accounting? 20; Detecting
creative accounting 22

2. **Fixed Assets**   24
Capital expenditure 25; Depreciation method 26;
Non-depreciating assets 28; Revaluation 29; Permanent
diminution in value 33

3. **Current Assets**   33
Stocks 33; Debtors 41; Cash 45

4. **Liabilities**   51
The liabilities that are on the balance sheet 52;
Off-balance sheet liabilities 58

5. **Income**   69
The arbitrariness of the accounting period 71;
Long-term contracts 72; Bad debt provision revisited 73;
Other problems of revenue recognition 74; Revenue
or capital? 77; Innovative financial instruments 78

6. **Expenses**   80
The price-earnings ratio 81; Deferred expenditure 82;
Capitalisation 83; Research and development 84;
Goodwill 85; Patents and trademarks 85; Provisions 86;
Reserve accounting 88; Extraordinary or
exceptional? 88; Changes in accounting policy and
prior year items 90

7. Mergers and Takeovers 92
How mergers and takeovers differ 93; Preparing
for action 95; Accounting after a takeover 97;
Goodwill 98; Merger accounting 102

8. Tax 104
Tax avoidance 104; Timing differences 106;
Permanent differences 108; Creative accounting
and tax minimisation 110

9. Foreign Currencies 113
Transaction exposure 113; Translation exposure 115;
Which rate to use 117; Reserve accounting
revisited 118; Functional currencies of
subsidiaries 119; Choosing the currency for
a transaction 120

10. Special Purpose Creative Accounting 121
Budgets 122; Actuals 125; Moving costs around 126;
Moving costs between years 127; Explaining
variances 128; Capital budgeting 129; Transfer
pricing 132

11. The Presentation 135
Administration costs 135; Intangible fixed assets 136;
Accounting policies 137; Associated companies 138;
Inflation accounting 141; Creative statistics 144

Epilogue: Is the Situation Getting Better or Worse? 146

Appendix: Summary of Statements of Standard 151
Accounting Practice issued by the
Accounting Standards Committee

Further Reading from Kogan Page 156

Index 157

Chapter 1
Accounting and Creative Accountancy

Introduction

ACCOUNTING HAS SOMEHOW acquired the reputation of being a highly impartial and objective process—the result of well-known and established rules which can always be relied on to produce the same result given the same set of facts or events. It is somewhat difficult to understand how it has acquired this reputation, especially among accountants, who above all know how far this characterisation differs from the reality of their daily professional lives. They know that a thousand different accountants, given the same facts, will come up with a thousand different sets of accounts—not wildly different, perhaps, but certainly not identical. Since accounting is a social science rather than a process that reflects the immutable laws of nature, this should not come as a surprise to anyone.

Perhaps it is the accounting profession itself that is to blame for this misperception. The usual picture that the general public has of an accountant is that he or she is precise, controlled, objective and reliable. This is probably the image that many, if not most, accountants wish for themselves, and is self-perpetuating in that it may well attract entrants to the profession that fit this description. The people create the myth and the myth attracts more defenders.

Yet, in reality, accounting is not like that except in the very simplest of situations. The accounting process consists of dealing with many matters of judgement and of resolving conflicts between competing approaches to the presentation of the results of financial events and transactions. One of the most important of these conflicts is between the opposing demands of relevance and

7

reliability. Or, to put it bluntly, should the accounts contain the information that is most likely to be of interest to the reader, even if it may not be 100 per cent reliable, or should they contain only that information that is known for certain to be true and completely verifiable? Neither of these extremes is achievable in practice, nor would either necessarily be desirable, but they do demonstrate one of the major judgemental areas that needs to be addressed by accountants.

It is this subjectivity and the need for judgement that is accounting's great strength and yet, at the same time, its great weakness. While, on the one hand, it needs to remain flexible enough to be able to cope with a wide variety of situations and represent them accurately in the accounts, on the other, this flexibility provides opportunities for manipulation, deceit and misrepresentation. These activities—practised by the less scrupulous elements of the accounting profession—have come to be known as 'creative accounting'.

It is, of course, neither creative nor is it proper accounting. It does not contribute to the generation of wealth in any way—at best it is a means of transferring wealth from those that are in the dark to those that are in the know. Nor is it accounting in any real sense since its objectives are *not* to represent things the way they really are but to show them the way someone wishes they were. There is a world of difference between the legitimate differences in accounting measurement and interpretation which reflect the real differences between companies and the cynical manipulation that is creative accounting.

The state of a business, its wealth and its profitability, cannot be observed directly. It needs to be represented in words, numbers and pictures if those who have an interest in its health and prospects are to find out what they want to know. This is the role of accounting. It is a language that describes and communicates aspects of a business to its owners and to other interested parties. Like any other language, it has its characteristic rules, nuances and shortcomings. The user of the language needs to be fully familiar with all these subtleties in order to know what is really being said and what is being left unsaid.

This book is about that language and how it is misused by the creative accountant. It will attempt to explain, first of all, something about the nature and the limitations of accounting. This, it is hoped, will enable the reader to understand more clearly what financial statements can and cannot convey and the difference between the public perception of accounts as unequivocal and true and the reality of their ambiguity and subjectivity.

Financial statements

Most sets of published accounts contain three main financial statements together with a set of notes which explain and amplify them. These statements are:

(a) the profit and loss account
(b) the balance sheet
(c) the source and use of funds statement.

Profit and loss account

As its name implies, the profit and loss account is intended to show how much richer or poorer the company has become during the period covered, which is usually a year. It shows not only the total amount of the profit or the loss for the year—the 'bottom line'— but also a considerable amount of detail about how that profit or loss has come about. It is often more useful to know what makes up the profit than simply to know the absolute amount of the profit itself.

The profit and loss account starts by showing the total turnover. This figure represents the total sales proceeds received from third parties during the year and is a measure of the company's level of activity during that period. From this is deducted the cost of the goods sold, giving the gross margin or trading profit. This figure measures the first level of the company's profitability and is often used to compare the operating efficiency of different companies.

The next cost to be deducted relates to indirect expenses—administration costs, overheads, the costs of research and development, and such items as maintenance and selling and marketing expenses. The amount remaining after deducting these costs is the profit before interest and taxes. Interest is regarded not so much as a cost of running the business but as a cost of providing it with capital by way of loans and mortgages. It represents the payment to the providers of loan capital for the use of their money in financing the operations of the company and is sometimes thought of as a first distribution of part of the company's profit to one of the principal providers of finance. Usually, the amount paid out is either predetermined or related to market interest rates and it must be paid whether or not there is a profit.

The taxation charge which is deducted next is the amount that the company expects to have to pay in tax in respect of the accounting profits of the period. Some of it may not have to be paid immediately—deferred tax—and some may never have to be paid at all if the company's tax advisers have their way. Calculating the amount that should be charged against each year's profit is one of the most difficult areas of accounting and, as we shall see later, provides plenty of scope for creative accounting.

After deducting interest and tax, any costs that are not considered typical of the year in question or which relate to previous years are deducted. These are known as 'extraordinary items' and, because they are not taken into account when calculating certain key ratios, they are of considerable interest to creative accountants as we shall see later.

Finally, when all the year's costs have been deducted from the year's gross proceeds, the bottom line is the income that is potentially distributable to the shareholders as dividends. Not all of it will be paid out in this way since the company will probably want to retain a proportion for investment in expansion. That part of the current year's profit that is not distributed is added to the undistributed profits from previous years and remains in the balance sheet as retained earnings and reserves.

The layout of the profit and loss account sometimes leads inexpert readers to think that the income and expenses occur chronologically in the order in which they appear in the accounts. This is not necessarily the case—each day the business is buying and selling goods, incurring overheads such as rent and rates on the factory and paying the wages of the work-force. The layout of the profit and loss account is merely a logical device for representing all these activities in money terms—it doesn't mean that the transactions occur in that order. All accounting is only a representation in words and numbers of what has gone on in the business during a particular period. It allows the management and the shareholders to see a whole year's activity at one time.

It should also be understood that some of the sales revenue shown will not yet have been received in cash, nor will some of the bills representing costs and expenses have been paid. The profit and loss account does not represent the cash inflows and outflows that have occurred during the period—that is the role of the source and use of funds statement — but shows the economic activity that has occurred during the period. The company might well have become richer during the period, ie have made a profit without necessarily having more cash at the end of the period than it had at the beginning. It could have less or even none at all — it is the total of net assets that determines wealth and the change in net assets that measures profit, not cash alone.

Balance sheet

The main purpose of the balance sheet is to show the amount and composition of the net assets owned by the company at the end of the period. Most balance sheets are prepared under what is known as the historical cost convention which means that the values shown for assets and liabilities are the original costs of those assets or the amounts that the company originally incurred by way of liabilities. The amounts attributable to assets and liabilities under this convention do not, therefore, represent their values in an economic sense. The principle of prudence, which also underlies much financial reporting, means that the amounts shown for assets may not be higher than their values and the amounts shown for liabilities may not be lower than their historical amounts. The principle is not applied symmetrically, however, since there is no prohibition on understating assets or overstating liabilities. This is yet another opportunity for the creative accountant to get to work.

Because of these conventions, it will be seen that the conventional balance sheet is not a statement of values in the way that an individual might understand one and might wish to prepare one to establish his net worth. It is all the more confusing for the reader of the accounts that the balance sheet looks like a statement of values. It is necessary to remember, however, that the net assets in a conventional balance sheet have a conventional meaning not an intuitive one, although this is probably not properly understood by many of the users of financial statements.

The assets in the balance sheet are grouped into two main categories — fixed assets and current assets. Fixed assets are not fixed for ever, of course, but are those assets which have useful economic lives that are longer than an individual accounting period. Typically, they would be the factories, warehouses and offices owned by the company together with the plant and machinery installed in them. Fixed assets are not held by the company for resale but are used to produce the goods and services that the company sells to its customers.

Current assets are those which circulate in the business and are constantly used up and renewed or replaced. At the balance sheet date it is expected that they will have been consumed during the next accounting period. They include stocks of raw materials, work in progress and finished goods awaiting despatch to customers, and amounts of money owed by customers for goods that have been delivered to them but for which they have not yet paid. These amounts are known as debtors. Cash in hand and bank balances are also current assets.

Liabilities are amounts owed by the company to third parties and are divided into long-term liabilities and current liabilities. Long-term liabilities are loans made to the company which are not due for repayment during the next accounting period, and may not be due for repayment for many years. The interest on the loans, however, will be payable regularly, probably every six months. Current liabilities, on the other hand, are those that are due for payment during the next accounting period, for goods and services that have already been supplied. Quite often, by the time the accounts have been finalised and published, these liabilities have been paid off and replaced by others.

Provisions are also amounts that the company has set aside for future payments but these do not represent actual liabilities at the balance sheet date. This may be because the amount is not known for certain or it may be that the person to whom the payment is to be made is not yet known. Examples are amounts set aside for deferred taxation, where the actual amount can only be estimated and which is not an actual liability until the tax assessment is raised, or product warranties, where neither the amount nor the payee can be estimated with great accuracy at the balance sheet date. Some provisions do not represent payments in the future but reflect reductions in the values of assets such as obsolete stocks or amounts owed by debtors who are unable to pay, perhaps due to bankruptcy.

After all these liabilities and provisions have been deducted from the assets of the company, the balance is the total amounts of the net assets of the company. Usually, this is also known as the equity or the shareholders' funds and will often be divided into a number of categories. Share capital is one of these categories and represents the amount that the shareholders have contributed to the company by buying its shares. This amount is not affected by any changes in the market price of the company's shares since it only relates to the amount subscribed by the original or subsequent shareholders who bought shares from the company, and is also unaffected by share dealings between shareholders.

A second category of shareholders' funds is retained earnings which, as mentioned earlier, represent the proportion of profits that has not been distributed to shareholders by way of dividend but has been retained in the business to finance expansion. The balance sheet also usually contains a further category of shareholders' funds called reserves which may be further subdivided. Reserves are often profits which have not yet been realised, such as the increase in the value of properties owned and still used by the company, which need to be separately identified. One reason for the separate identification is that company law does not allow unrealised profits to be distributed as dividends.

Articulation of the profit and loss account and balance sheet

The universally used method of keeping accounting records is known as double-entry bookkeeping. This requires that every transaction has two aspects and requires two entries in the accounting records to reflect these aspects. For example, the purchase of trading stock for cash reduces the balance at the bank and, at the same time, increases the value of stock by the same amount. Also, when stock is sold to the final customer the sales price is added to the total of sales in the profit and loss account and the amount owed by the customer is added to the value of debtors in the balance sheet. The double-entry mechanism therefore ensures that the profit and loss account and the balance sheet both reflect the transaction and stay in line with one another. In accountants' jargon, the profit and loss account and the balance sheet are said to articulate with each other.

This means that, at the end of the period, the shareholders' funds are equal to the opening shareholders' funds plus the profit for the year plus any unrealised profits that have gone straight to reserves less any dividend paid. This balancing act does not ensure that the accounts are correct, of course, but only that the transactions that have been recorded have been put through both the profit and loss account and the balance sheet. A completely false or erroneous entry could have been made or an entry could have been omitted. When the profit and loss account and the balance sheet do not balance, however, the accountant can be sure that something is wrong.

Statement of source and use of funds

As mentioned earlier, the profit and loss account reflects economic activity during the period and this will not necessarily correspond with movements in cash and other funds. The information about this aspect of the business is provided by the statement of source and use of funds.

This statement usually starts with the bottom line of the profit and loss account, ie the profit after interest and taxation. It could just as easily start with details of the payments to suppliers and from customers, but the usual format allows the reader of the accounts to see how the cash flows relate to the profit for the period. This profit is then adjusted for items that have been taken into account in arriving at it but which do not involve movements in cash. Examples of these adjustments are depreciation and provisions for bad debts which, although they are costs to the business, have not themselves given rise to cash flows.

Next, the flow of funds into or out of working capital is analysed. Working capital comprises the amount invested by the business to keep it ticking over and consists of debtors, stock and cash, less creditors. For example, as the business expands and stock and debtors increase, more cash is tied up in as yet unsold goods until the purchase price is received from the customers. This cash outflow can be offset, at least partly, by an increase in creditors, ie by not having to pay straight away for the additional stockholding level.

The next major cash flow item is capital expenditure; that is the amount spent on purchasing new fixed assets and other net new investment. Any additional equity finance raised or any new loans taken out in the period are also shown in the source and use of funds statement, together with any repayments.

The bottom line on this statement will represent the net movements in cash or near-cash in the period. This amount will usually be quite different from the profit figure and could easily be negative even when a profit has been made or positive in spite of a loss. For example, a company that had sold a subsidiary during the period for less than it had paid for it could report a significant loss for the period in the profit and loss account but show a significant cash inflow due to the receipt of the sales proceeds. The statement of source and use of funds is intended to show where the cash has come from and where it has gone to in the period. Its importance is a reflection of the fact that more companies come unstuck due to cash flow problems than from lack of profitability although, in the long run, a company needs both to be profitable and to turn those profits into cash if it is to survive and prosper.

The objectives of accounting

These, then, are the main financial statements which are usually supplemented by a series of notes containing explanations and additional details about particular items. Their objectives seem straightforward: the profit and loss account shows the profit or the loss; the balance sheet shows the assets, liabilities and share-holders' funds; and the statement of source and use of funds shows the cash flows. In practice, however, the objectives of financial statements have become more complex in recent years as the vol-ume and complexity of disclosure have increased and as the users of financial statements have become more demanding. Accounts are no longer simply a report on past activity and current solvency—the so-called 'stewardship' function of financial reporting. Today, investors and other users of accounts expect to be able to use them to foresee a company's future and to forecast its profitability.

Even when accounts were used primarily for assessing the past performance of management there was incentive enough to mass-age the accounts. The additional emphasis on their predictive abil-ity adds to this incentive particularly if this helps to avoid any unwelcome volatility in the profits from one period to the next. As we shall see, a great deal of creative accounting effort goes into ensuring that optimistic conclusions can be—and will be—drawn from the numbers shown in the accounts.

The limitations of accounting

The problem with all this is that historical cost accounting is not really up to producing numbers which are necessarily appropriate for forecasting, being strongly influenced by the traditional accounting virtues of prudence and consistency. In fact, they are not very good, as we have already discovered, at showing current values, so it should not be all that surprising that they are not particularly useful for predicting future values. From the tension produced by the difference between the expectations of the users of accounts and what accounts can actually deliver comes the phenomenon of creative accounting.

Over the full life of a company, of course, there will be no doubt as to the amount of profits or losses it has made. When the company is finally wound up the amount returned to the shareholders, plus the dividends they have received, can be compared to the amount they originally invested in the company and the difference is the profit or the loss. In the early days of accounting this is exactly what happened; only when a venture was completed was the accounting done and the participants were paid out in proportion to their investment in the venture. However, as commercial and industrial enterprises became more complex and more long-lived, investors became less inclined to wait until they were wound up to be paid out and came to expect periodic accounting and periodic dividends based on those accounts. Nowadays, most major and many smaller industrial and commercial companies can expect to have a practically indefinite life, and financial accounting cannot rely on a final wind-up to prove its accuracy. It is expected to be as accurate as possible every year.

The longer lives of commercial and industrial companies are often reflected in longer business cycles and longer-lived assets. Many large companies are engaged in long-term projects and have assets which will last for 50 years or more. This is particularly true of the oil, mining and construction industries, for example. This long cycle makes it difficult to allocate costs and revenues to particular years and adds another element of judgement and subjectivity to the reporting of income. How long does an oil refinery last? When is profit actually earned on a five-year-long dam construction project? Will the cost of an investment actually pay off and, if not, how much loss should be recognised now and how much next year?

Another area where judgement is required concerns how much detail to put into financial statements. The day-to-day process of bookkeeping is concerned with recording transactions, as they occur, in great detail. The payroll is calculated to the nearest penny, the detail has to be correct for every employee and the costs have to be allocated over factories, offices, departments, products and processes. Each invoice that is sent out is recorded individually as is each invoice received, stock records are kept by individual

item and separate, detailed accounts are maintained for each customer and each supplier. Expenses are analysed and charged to
cost centres and allocations and apportionments of common costs
are made on a variety of bases.

Clearly, it would not be feasible to present to the shareholders at
the end of each year a complete detailed record of every transaction undertaken and every allocation made. Not only would such
an account be very voluminous but it would also be very difficult
to interpret. Financial statements are intended to represent, in a
simplified form, all the transactions and allocations that have
occurred during the period and the resulting financial position at
the end of the period. They do this by summarising and aggregat-
ing similar transactions under standardised headings. In the UK,
the layout of financial statements is governed by the Companies
Act 1985, but considerable discretion remains with individual
companies as to what is actually included under each heading.

The rules

The existence of these areas of discretion and judgement does not
mean, of course, that financial reporting is a free-for-all and that
there are no rules at all. Over the years a considerable number of
general rules has emerged from accounting practice and they have
become generally accepted. The accounting profession has always
taken considerable pride in its ability to generate and maintain
professional standards at both the technical and the ethical levels.
These technical rules cannot, however, cover every eventuality
and every situation nor are they intended to. They are expressed in
fairly general terms and reflect the fact that every enterprise is
slightly different and a certain degree of flexibility is necessary if
accounting is not to be forced into a strait-jacket. Over the last 20
years or so, the previously nebulous body of generally accepted
accounting rules has become rather more well defined through
both the actions of the accounting profession itself and through
legislation in the UK and the European Community.

In the accounting profession, the question of dealing with the
variety of accounting practices changed from being an internal
and somewhat esoteric concern of professional accountants primarily to being, in the mid-1960s, a major business scandal. A
number of individual events, including the collapse of Rolls Razor
and the GEC-AEI take-over, pushed creative accounting firmly

into the spotlight. This was particularly critical in the case of AEI which made an optimistic profit forecast in its defence to the bid from GEC. In the event, this forecast was not met, not because of a downturn in its fortunes but because the accounting methods used by GEC after the takeover were markedly different from those used by AEI. When this became common knowledge, the confidence of the public in the neutrality of accounting suffered a severe blow. Concern was expressed that, if the accounting profession could not or would not do something to reform the process of financial reporting, then perhaps the government should step in.

The largest and most influential of the UK accounting bodies, the Institute of Chartered Accountants in England and Wales had, for many years, produced accounting recommendations on a number of difficult topics. It was generally believed that these recommendations were being followed but the Institute had no real mechanism for monitoring or enforcement. More important, perhaps, at least for the public perception of the accountability of the profession, the process of developing these recommendations was a private one. It was largely an internal matter between individual chartered accountants and the Institute, and the wording of some of the recommendations was vague enough to be able to accommodate the passage of the proverbial coach and horses.

In response to these problems, and especially the threat that the government might take the initiative in setting detailed accounting standards, the profession established what is now called the Accounting Standards Committee (ASC). Initially, it consisted only of accountants but it has been expanded in recent years and now has non-accountant members and non-voting observers. The ASC produces Statements of Standard Accounting Practice, known as SSAPs, which are intended to be mandatory although they do not actually have the force of law. SSAPs are enforced principally through the disciplinary procedures of the accounting institutes which require their members to comply with them whether they act as directors or auditors. Where they are not complied with, perhaps because they do not apply or where their application would give a false or misleading picture, the accounts should state this non-compliance together with the reasons for it. Auditors are required to ensure that companies comply or state why they do not and must either agree with the non-compliance or qualify the accounts.

SSAPs are of rather variable quality both as regards their conceptual merit and their ability to reduce the variety of accounting treatment and to stamp out the more questionable practices. While some are clear and unequivocal, others are dubious and vague. Their success in dealing with the problem of creative accounting has been limited. This is perhaps not all that surprising since SSAPs are produced and enforced entirely outside the realm of the law, although they are probably now becoming absorbed into the law as part of general custom and practice. When, however, an essentially voluntary process that relies on goodwill and pragmatism comes up against entrenched views and sectional interests, one should not be too surprised if the occasional fudged compromise emerges. A summary of the full list of current SSAPs is provided in the Appendix.

Accounting regulation in the UK is not, however, left entirely to the accounting profession. For many years the Companies Acts have contained requirements as to the preparation and publication of accounts. Until relatively recently the contents of these accounts and their method of presentation were not specified in detail in the law but in the last few years the legislation has become more detailed and specific and thus more prescriptive. Consolidated accounts for groups of companies were not required until the 1948 Act and the 1981 Act (now the 1985 Act) set out required formats and valuation rules. Even the current legal rules are not as detailed and prescriptive as are required in many other countries but the trend would seem to be clear. We can expect more regulation rather than less, particularly if the accounting profession and the business community are unwilling or unable to deal with problems as they arise and particularly under a government less inclined to self-regulation than the present one.

There is considerable evidence that the accounting profession and the wider business community *are* concerned about the variety of accounting practices and the development of creative accounting and are prepared to act to improve matters. The existence of this book is one small example of this concern. Another is the effort currently being put into the development of non-mandatory Statements of Recommended Practice (SORPs) which are intended to remove some of the scope for creative accounting in particular industries. The oil industry and the insurance industry have taken the lead in this process but others are not far behind.

What is creative accounting?

Creative accounting is not against the law. It operates within the letter both of the law and of accounting standards but it is quite clearly against the spirit of both. It should also be remembered that creative accounting is not necessarily practised only by dishonest or corrupt accountants and crooked company directors. This is one of the aspects that makes it difficult to deal with. It is essentially a process of using the rules, the flexibility provided by them and the omissions within them, to make financial statements look somewhat different from what was intended by the rule. It consists of rule-bending and loophole-seeking.

It includes the process by which transactions are structured so as to produce the required accounting outcome rather than allowing accounting to report transactions in a neutral and consistent way. It has given rise to two particularly unpleasant and insidious practices—standards avoidance and opinion-shopping. *Standards avoidance* is the financial reporting equivalent of tax avoidance—legal, but designed to thwart the objectives of the law-maker. *Opinion-shopping* refers to the practice of asking a number of firms of auditors about their attitude to a particular accounting treatment or practice—usually a questionable one. As competition increases in the somewhat static audit market, the latter practice, which is clearly intended to encourage auditors to turn a blind eye in order to obtain a particular audit appointment, is likely to become increasingly common.

Let there be no doubt about it, creative accounting is a bad thing. It distorts company results and financial position and, if the theorists are to be believed, this leads to inefficient allocations in the economy.

Why then does creative accounting happen? The protagonists, if you could find any who would admit to being supporters of creative accounting, would probably argue that it is forced on them by the users of accounts in general and the City in particular. They would claim that most financial analysts and other commentators have a fixation about a few key ratios and numbers in the accounts and that they are too ignorant or too lazy to make a real effort to deepen their understanding of business beyond these. They like to see steady progress in net income, earnings per share, etc and react badly if a company announces results that are markedly different from the market's expectations. This, it is argued, coupled with a short-term emphasis whereby analysts are only interested in the financial results for the current year and the next year, forces a company that does not want to fall out with its shareholders and their advisers to do what they demand.

The more hawkish would go even further and observe that, while the analysts claim to be acting in the best interests of current and future investors, in fact their own interests conflict with those of these groups. Their interests relate to the commissions that their firms earn on buying and selling shares and thus they are much more interested in identifying 'buy' and 'sell' recommendations than in 'hold' recommendations. They therefore take more interest in variations from the steady state than in the norm and spend their professional life seeking out overpriced and underpriced shares. In such an environment, a sudden increase in profits can be as embarrassing as a sudden reduction if it creates inflated expectations about the results of future periods which cannot be met.

Creative accountants might also argue that, in the long run, their activities are limited to income-smoothing since many creative accounting techniques rebound fairly quickly. That is, a trick that increases income this year has the effect of reducing it next year. Thus, it might be argued that creative accounting is in the best interests of the shareholders since it protects them from the vagaries of the more speculative elements in the financial markets.

Such claims smack of after-the-event rationalisations but they do contain more than a grain of truth. The City is often criticised— and not only by its enemies—for its short-term view and for the conflicts of interest that exist in some City institutions and which have survived recent improvements in the system of self-regulation. A more educated and informed body of shareholders would no doubt help the process but this is not something that can happen overnight. In the meantime, books like this can help by explaining the nature and process of creative accounting and by promoting the realisation that even the best in accounting is an art rather than a science and depends on goodwill and co-operation to achieve its objectives.

It is important that accounting does not become too hidebound by restrictive rules and detailed prescription since such approaches will only generate even more effort to beat the system. The effort and skill that go into the avoidance of tax is an obvious and depressing parallel. The accounting framework should remain flexible and should retain enough scope for all companies to be accommodated in one system in a broadly comparable manner, but not so flexible as to allow the financial statements of our leading companies to qualify for the Booker Prize.

Detecting creative accounting

Detecting creative accounting without help is very difficult. Equally difficult is the process of adjusting creatively produced accounts on to a more reasonable basis. The main source of information about how the accounts have been put together and what scope there has been for creative accounting should be provided by the statement of accounting policies that all companies are expected to produce in accordance with the requirements of SSAP 2.

It would be naive, however, to expect that an accountant or a board of directors that had put a great deal of effort into creative accounting would then go and blow their own cover by disclosing what they had done and how it could be spotted in the statement of accounting policies. Even in the best companies the accounting policies statement usually sounds rather bland and vague. This is not necessarily an attempt to be obscure but is more likely to reflect the view that this part of the accounts is as much of a bore to prepare as it is to read. Furthermore, since it takes up useful space that is usually at a premium in most sets of accounts, there is considerable pressure to condense it as much as possible.

If one is really serious about spotting creative accounting, however, this is definitely the first place to look. However vague the wording, the auditors will not allow clearly untrue statements to remain in this section, so what is there can be relied upon to be factually correct. The curious reader should compare the wording of the description of each accounting policy with the wording of the relevant accounting standard (SSAP) and query any obvious discrepancies. Quite often the financial press will start this process off and the *Financial Times* has a good—although not perfect—record in this area. The journal of the Institute of Chartered Accountants in England and Wales, called *Accountancy*, is also a useful source of information on suspicious accounting methods—even ones that have satisfied their auditors' scrutiny.

Making the necessary adjustments requires, in practice, a thorough knowledge of the industry in question or the assistance of the company. Stockbrokers can often help with the first of these but the second source of assistance is not usually forthcoming. When one is tackling creative accounting one has to be prepared to plough a lone furrow most of the time. The only advice that can be offered is be suspicious, persistent and beware. And good hunting!

Chapter 2
Fixed Assets

FOR THOSE CREATIVE accountants who wish to transform the balance sheet from what it actually is to what they would like it to be the starting point is often the fixed assets section. This, as explained in Chapter 1, is the group of assets that provides the main productive capacity of the business. They are fixed in the sense that they are longer lived than most other assets and stay in use in the company for many years. This does not mean, of course, that they last for ever—although, as we shall see, some of the more creative accountants seem to be claiming that they never wear out.

Fixed assets must be depreciated over their useful economic lives. Deciding what actually is the useful economic life of a particular fixed asset is a matter of business judgement and, therefore, provides a significant opportunity for creative accounting. Many company directors are not members of professional accounting bodies and many will have no sympathy with the objectives of the Accounting Standards Committee and other accounting standard setters. They will, quite naturally, be principally concerned with the interests of their company and may regard standard setters as interfering busybodies who simply get in the way of making a profit. If they think about the wider public interest at all, they may content themselves with the thought that 'what is good for Bloggs Industries is good for Britain'. Thus, the accountants in a company, even if they do not start out to be creative, may come under pressure from the very top echelons in a company.

Perhaps the first thing to remember about accounting for fixed assets is that the amount at which they are shown in the balance sheet does not necessarily represent their value. In fact it usually won't, but will generally be a mixture of variously calculated amounts for each individual asset or group of assets. In most cases,

the basis will be historical cost, that is, the amount that was paid
for the asset when it was originally purchased, or, where the assets
were constructed by the company itself, the cost of production.
The latter situation will provide plenty of opportunities for creative accounting as we shall see.

Capital expenditure

The expenditure on fixed assets, or capital expenditure, is not written off immediately against profits but is carried forward in the
balance sheet and depreciated over the *useful life* of the asset purchased. Useful economic life will not usually be the same as the
technical life since a piece of plant or machinery might well continue to run successfully and produce satisfactory output long
after it has ceased to be able to do so economically. One method of
determining useful economic life would be to forecast the cash
flows that are expected to occur in the future as a direct conse-
quence of owning the asset, including the revenue it will earn and
the cost of replacement parts and any other maintenance that it
will need to keep it running. At the point where additional revenue
exceeds additional costs the useful economic life of the asset has
ended and it should be scrapped and replaced.

In practice, it is rare for an evaluation of this sort to take place.
The usual excuse would be that it is too difficult to do or that it
relies too much on subjective estimates to be useful. The real
reason is often that the useful life decision is taken by determining
first, what answer is required and second, by assessing what useful life will give that answer. If the company wishes to maintain its
fixed asset values in the balance sheet at the highest figures it can,
then the useful economic life will be as long as possible. If, on the
other hand, the company wishes to see its fixed asset values reducing quickly, it will choose much shorter useful economic lives.

The constraints on this decision will be set by precedent and by
the attitude of the auditors, and these are closely related to one
another. Clearly, an individual company cannot have widely differing useful economic lives for broadly similar assets and, in practice, useful economic lives will not be established for each individual
asset but for groups of them. The more categories of fixed assets a
company has, the more scope there is for claiming that a new asset
or group is different from existing groups and should have a different life. The auditors will try to make sure that there are no glaring

discrepancies, but as new technology develops it becomes easier for the management to differentiate between categories and to justify a variety of lives for assets that might seem similar.

Once the useful economic life has been set for an asset or group of assets this does not mean that it cannot be changed. In theory, a company can change the lives of its assets at any time and, indeed, the accounting standard on depreciation, SSAP 12, encourages companies to review asset lives regularly. By implication, if lives are thought to have changed, then this should be reflected in the accounting.

Auditors will, of course, become suspicious if this happens too often or if the result of the change seems to have convenient results for the profit and loss account. If this process is handled discreetly, in a low-key manner, and if the rationale is well presented, even the most hawkish auditor will have the utmost difficulty in sustaining an objection. Judicious manipulation of asset lives can, therefore, offer considerable scope for creative accounting among the fixed assets.

Depreciation method

Another means of massaging the fixed asset values in the balance sheet relates to the choice of the depreciation method. The most common method and the most easily understood is the straight line method. Under this approach, the fixed asset cost, less any scrap or salvage value, is allocated evenly over the useful economic life. A number of other methods exist, however, which will give a quite different pattern of allocation and therefore a different pattern of balance sheet values. Possible alternatives are the reducing-balance method by which a constant percentage of the opening value of the asset is written off each year, or the annuity method under which an increasing amount is written off each year. A further alternative is the unit-of-production method which is often used in the extractive industries and under which the amount of depreciation written off in each period is proportional to the production in that period. The effect of each of these alternatives is demonstrated in the following table which is based on an asset cost of £100,000, an asset life of ten years and production of 20,000 units in the first year, 30,000 in years 2 to 8 and 10,000 in each of the last two years:

Year	Straight line	25% Reducing balance	Annuity	Unit of production
1	90,000	75,000	93,726	92,000
2	80,000	56,250	86,825	80,000
3	70,000	42,188	79,233	68,000
4	60,000	31,640	70,882	56,000
5	50,000	23,730	61,695	44,000
6	40,000	17,797	51,590	32,000
7	30,000	13,348	40,475	20,000
8	20,000	10,011	28,247	8,000
9	10,000	7,508	14,796	4,000
10	—	5,631	—	—

As will be obvious from the above, the balance sheet value for the asset will depend considerably on the depreciation method used. Equally, the conclusions that can be drawn from the balance sheet value are dependent on an understanding of the depreciation method and how it affects the pattern of the balance sheet. For example, if the user of the accounts wanted to assess how much of the useful economic life of the above asset remained at the end of year 5, he might think that it was anything from less than a quarter to two-thirds depending on which depreciation method had been used by the company. Where a company uses a variety of methods and changes some of them from time to time, it is practically impossible to make any sense of the balance sheet values of the fixed assets.

However, changing depreciation methods is usually more difficult to justify to auditors and shareholders than simply changing asset lives, although it can be done in moderation as a subtle means of manipulating fixed asset values. Sometimes the objective will be profit manipulation rather than balance sheet manipulation since the depreciation charge is deducted from profit. Whatever the motive, it is unlikely that the user of the accounts will detect it unless it is so material that the auditors insist that the effect is disclosed separately. When this happens it may be necessary for the creative accountant to leave depreciation alone for a while. This will probably not worry him unduly since he has many more weapons in his creative armoury with which to confuse and confound the unprepared user of his accounts.

Non-depreciating assets

One of these other weapons is to convince himself, the board of directors and the auditors that some of the company's assets do not need depreciating at all. The directors may not take much persuading, particularly if the fixed assets in question are property. They will know from personal experience that the value of property tends to increase continually under the influence of inflation and in response to the effects of demand and supply. While some of them may remember the property crash of the early 1970s it would be a brave accountant who suggested to them that the company's property was not appreciating, let alone that it was reducing in value.

The auditors may be a little more difficult to persuade, but the legal rules and the accounting standards provide plenty of scope in this area. The Companies Act only requires depreciation to be deducted from assets that have a finite economic life, and the accounting standard SSAP 12 allows specifically for freehold land not to be depreciated. Many companies extend this exemption to the buildings as well, arguing that they have an infinite economic life since they are continually maintained and brought up to date. This means, of course, that the profit and loss account has to bear the cost of the maintenance but this will not be a problem if balance sheet enhancement is the main objective. It might even be possible to argue that some of the maintenance expenditure represents improvements to the property and that it should be capitalised rather than written off to the profit and loss account. This will often be a difficult point to argue but, on the other hand, it can be equally difficult for the auditor to deny and often much that is truly maintenance expense is surreptitiously capitalised in this way. Besides, it takes more than the prospect of a vigorous argument to put the creative accountant off.

It is not usually possible, however, to argue that fixed assets other than property have infinite useful economic lives and do not need depreciating. Very few items of plant can avoid physical deterioration and, even if they could—through rigorous maintenance, for example—they would inevitably become technologically obsolete in the long run. Occasionally, companies do get away with not depreciating non-property assets; a notable example is newspaper titles and publishing imprints where it is argued that these assets retain their value in attracting customers and authors and should not be written off. Sometimes the creative accountant will go so far as to plead that these assets should not be written off in the public interest since to do so will make the publishers look poorer than they really are and will attract unwelcome take-over bids, perhaps from abroad. Where companies have been able to persuade themselves and their auditors that they do possess such assets, it will almost certainly be necessary for them to disclose this in the notes, particularly the accounting policies note. Detectives of creative accounting should scan the notes carefully for disclosures of this sort since this kind of accounting can hardly be said to correspond very closely to business or economic reality.

Revaluation

The next step from claiming that some of the assets have not declined in value is to assert that some of them have actually increased in value. In some ways this is rather more believable than the infinite life claim since it is clear that some assets do increase in value over time, seemingly without ever ceasing to do so. Property is the example that springs immediately to mind; there are other assets that go up in value but few do so as consistently as property. When it is clear that an increase in value has occurred, the scope for massaging the balance sheet is considerable since there are two variables that can be introduced into the creative accounting process—the amount of the revaluation and the timing of its recognition. Potentially, there is also a third— whether the revalued amount or the original historical cost amount should be used as the basis for depreciation, although this has now effectively been ruled out by the latest version of SSAP 12.

But first, the revaluation itself. When a revaluation occurs and this is reflected in the accounts, there are two aspects that are reflected in the double-entry bookkeeping system: the asset value in the balance sheet is increased by the amount of the revaluation, and this increase, which represents an unrealised profit, is added to the reserves included in the shareholders' funds section of the balance sheet. This profit cannot be included in the profit and loss account until it has been realised by a sale and cannot be distributed to shareholders as dividend.

To many readers of the accounts this is a strange kind of profit. While it is, perhaps, nice to know that the company's resources have been invested in an asset that has increased in value, if this asset is one that the company needs to use in order to produce goods and services for resale, the company can hardly benefit from this increase in value. Moreover, if this new increased value is used for depreciation purposes, as the revised version of SSAP 12 says it should, the effect of this increase in value will be to reduce future profits. This might seem eminently logical, but one can be sure that the creative accountant will wish to benefit from the increased value without having to suffer the disadvantages.

Having one's cake in this context consists of the improvement that the revaluation has on the balance sheet. The asset values will have increased as a result of the revaluation and so will shareholders' funds. Where the balance sheet contains borrowings, the increase in shareholders' funds will be 'geared', ie they will increase proportionately more than the assets. So far, so good.

Eating one's cake as well consists of ensuring that the corresponding adverse effect on the profit and loss account is avoided or, at least, minimised. Even if the increased depreciation cannot be avoided, the accounts will look better for some time until the additional charge has eaten away the increased asset value. But it may be possible to delay the effect even longer by combining a revaluation with an increase in the asset life so as to reduce the annual depreciation charge. It will be even better, though, if the revaluation can be confined to non-depreciating assets so that there is no offsetting additional depreciation.

Split depreciation

Where, however, the revaluation is made to a depreciating asset and there is no scope for changing the asset life, a little more creativity is called for. It was under just such circumstances that Woolworths invented what came to be known as 'split depreciation'. Woolworths had revalued their shop properties by a significant amount as part of a general overhaul of what had been an underperforming company that owned enormously valuable high street sites. In order to avoid having to take the resulting increase in the depreciation charge to the profit and loss account, Woolworths split it into the portion that related to the original, historical cost and that which related to the revaluation adjustment. The former portion they charged to the profit and loss account and the latter to the revaluation reserve in shareholders' funds. So, while the balance sheet benefited from the increase in the value of the properties, the profit and loss account was only charged with the same amount of depreciation that it would have been had the revaluation not taken place.

This treatment provoked considerable controversy in the accounting and business world. Its proponents contended that it was quite logical and was not motivated by the desire to be creative. The essence of their argument was that since the unrealised profit on the revaluation did not go through the profit and loss account, it was only logical that the depreciation on this profit should also be excluded from the profit and loss account. The split depreciation method, they claimed, provided symmetry where the more conventional method did not and it was, therefore, a preferable method of accounting.

The ASC was not convinced, however, and the revised version of SSAP 12 outlawed this practice. It now requires that the depreciation charge should not only be based on the balance sheet value but should all be charged to the profit and loss account. The conceptual basis for this assertion is by no means well founded and the ASC did not attempt to put a theoretical argument forward in support of its decision. It seems likely that this issue is not dead, particularly since there is considerable doubt as to whether this aspect of SSAP 12 could successfully withstand a legal challenge.

Whether or not split depreciation is a goner, there is still considerable life left in revaluations as a source of balance sheet revitalisation. The actual amount by which assets are revalued is often a very contentious issue. Valuation is a subjective process at the best of times and quite different valuations of the same assets could emerge depending on the particular assumptions used by the valuer. Where there is a wide range in the valuations of a particular asset—and these can arise for quite legitimate reasons—the question arises as to which valuation should be used for the accounts and how is an auditor to be satisfied that the chosen value is appropriate? It is, in practice, very difficult to argue with a valuation prepared by a qualified chartered surveyor and few auditors would be prepared to go to the expense of having another valuation, particularly if it is not possible to recover the cost in the audit fee. It is not unknown for a company to ask for a valuation from a number of surveyors and then to use the one that produces the required result from an accounting point of view. Only where a valuation is obviously and outrageously wrong can it be challenged by the auditors and, even then, this may not occur.

Companies are not under any obligation to revalue and where

they do, they are not forced to do so regularly although this is encouraged. In practice, the directors have almost complete freedom to revalue by as much or as little and as often as they wish, or to refrain from revaluing when it does not suit them. They are required, however, to provide some details of revaluations but this is not much of a safeguard against abuse since such statements are difficult to interpret for users of accounts who do not know the background to the revaluations and why they have or have not occurred.

It cannot be coincidence that revaluations occur most often when companies are under threat from take-overs. Actually, it is not companies themselves that are threatened by take-overs so much as their boards of directors. Since the argument between the directors of the offeror company and those of the offeree company is most often about financial performance and share values, it is not surprising that the boosting of the balance sheet becomes a preoccupation of the defending board. In such circumstances it may be their jobs and their way of life that are really at stake.

Sometimes, however, creative accounting for fixed assets comes into its own after a take-over has been completed. Having made such a song and dance about the incompetence of the outgoing board, the new board will usually be at pains to ensure that its performance is better—at least, as far as it is reflected in the accounts. Whether the company had indulged in revaluations before it was taken over or not, the new owners might decide that a downward revaluation is in order after the take-over. One reason for doing this might be to discredit the outgoing board and this use of accounting shows that it is as much a political tool as an economic one. Another reason might be to reduce subsequent depreciation charges and boost future profits. The reduction in asset values would further increase future measures of return on capital employed.

Also, the write-down in asset values need not even necessarily be put through the profit and loss account if the balance sheet already contains a previous revaluation surplus on the same assets against which it can be charged. Even where such a write-down has to be taken against profits, the blame can be laid at the door of the previous management.

Permanent diminution in value

The final area for creative accounting in the fixed asset part of the balance sheet is, almost incredibly, provided explicitly by the Companies Act. The 1985 Act requires that a provision be made where permanent diminution in value of a fixed asset has occurred. What is more, the Act also requires that where the conditions that persuaded the directors that permanent diminution had occurred in the first place no longer apply, the provision must be written back to the extent that it is no longer needed. A creative accountant's charter if ever there was one!

On the basis of this provision, therefore, creative accountants can decrease or increase the balance sheet amounts for fixed assets at will so long as they can persuade that permanent diminution in value has — or even might have — occurred or that it has gone away. This provision could almost be read to allow depreciation that has been provided in the past to be written back to profit and loss account, although no such practice has been spotted as yet and the revised version of SSAP 12 seems to prohibit it except in exceptional circumstances. If it is happening, it is being kept well hidden, but then many of creative accounting's more useful ploys lose much of their effectiveness if they become too well known.

So it would appear that fixed assets enjoy anything but fixed accounting treatment. The backbone of the balance sheet is, in fact, as flexible as that of a limbo dancer. The accounting rules that seem so rigid in the textbooks are, in reality, open to considerable manipulation. But this is only the beginning. Many creative accountants can conjure up the accounts they wish without even venturing into this part of the balance sheet, as we shall discover.

Chapter 3
Current Assets

ACCOUNTING FOR CURRENT assets should be pretty straightforward—according to the law, that is. The Companies Act 1985 states clearly that, unless a company uses current cost accounting—and almost none do—its current assets should be shown in the balance sheet at cost or market value, if lower.

What could be simpler or more straightforward? Cost is cost, you might say. Everyone knows what is meant by that and even the auditors should be able to check up on that and make sure there is no creative accounting in this area without any great difficulty. Cost is what you have paid for something—just look up the purchase invoice and check that the amount recorded in the accounts is correct. However, as the reader will already have begun to suspect, nothing is quite that simple where there is a determination to produce the required result and even the apparently simple concept of cost can become very complicated. In order to look at the variety of accounting and presentational possibilities that exists for current assets, we shall look at each of them in turn: stocks and work in progress, debtors and cash. (Cash? Is it really possible legally to manipulate accounting for cash? Wait and see!)

Stocks

Companies carry all sorts of stocks for all sorts of reasons. Manufacturing companies will have stocks of raw materials for their production processes, bought-in components for subsequent assembly, stocks of partly completed products, known as work in progress, and stocks of finished products awaiting shipment to customers. In addition, there will be stocks of consumable items such as fuel, packaging materials, stationery, etc and stocks of by-products and scrap awaiting disposal. Some stocks will have been bought from outside suppliers and some will have been created directly or indirectly during the process of production. However the stocks have been produced, the determination of their cost will often be more of an art than a science and the results will depend greatly on the methods applied.

Why manipulate stocks anyway? What is the point? The basic point to remember is that, other things being equal, the higher the stock at the end of the year, the higher the profit for the year and the better the balance sheet looks. However, it should also be remembered that this year's closing stock is next year's opening stock so that the more this year's profit is flattered by a creatively increased stock figure, the more next year's profit is reduced. So the manipulation of stock values is an ideal method of profit-smoothing—either boosting one year's profit or hiding an unexpected and embarrassingly high profit in that year. Profit-smoothing is one of the creative accountant's principal objectives since he cannot create profit where there is none, at least, not in the long run. He can, however, move profits from one year to another to create the desired impression of steady improvement which, it seems, is what the stock market likes to see.

How to massage stock
There are any number of methods of accounting for stock and even the most commonly used ones can give quite different results. Some methods include in the valuation only the direct, out-of-pocket cost of buying the stock, whereas others will include some or all of the additional costs of getting the stock into place and ready for sale or use. The range of costs that can be included in stocks can vary from simply the purchase (or production) cost plus the inward freight costs, to a full absorption of production and conversion overheads, warehousing and handling costs, and fixed production overheads. Sometimes, even general administration costs and the interest on the capital tied up in the stocks are included in the value at which the stocks are accounted. Let us take these items one at a time and look at what opportunities exist for manipulation.

Discounts
The basic cost of purchasing the items that go into stock is usually not in doubt and cannot, therefore, easily be massaged, although

there may be opportunities even here. For example, suppliers may offer trade and cash discounts either for larger orders or for early settlement. Cash discounts will usually be accounted separately from the cost of the stock and will be credited to a cash discounts receivable account. The rationale for doing this is that the early payment of bills involves an additional financing cost and that the discounts received as compensation for early payment should be separately identified so that they can be compared with the additional financing costs incurred. Trade discounts, however, are different; they are not given for early payment but to stimulate trade or to encourage high-volume orders. They are, therefore, a genuine reduction in the cost of buying the stock, not a compensation for paying for it earlier than necessary. Thus, the stock will usually be accounted for at the net-of-trade-discount level, ie after deducting trade discount.

This difference in the treatment of trade and cash discounts clearly provides an opportunity for some subtle manipulation. Where cash discounts are not accounted for separately but are deducted from the stock value, the value of stock in the balance sheet is reduced and the charge to the profit and loss account when it is used or sold will also be lower. As indicated above, this is not the usual treatment and auditors will usually—should usually—query it. Nevertheless, it can still be done, particularly if the amounts are not material. It is even easier if the invoice from the supplier does not state clearly which kind of discount is being offered and it has even been suggested that some creative accountants would go to the lengths of asking the supplier to make sure that his invoices remain suitably vague. A further refinement to this theme is to arrange for trade or cash discounts to be documented separately from the associated invoices so as to make the process of manipulation easier.

Freight costs

The inclusion of freight costs in stock valuations can also be a fruitful source of creativity in accounting for stock and can be very effective when the cost of freight is high compared with the value of the stock. The argument usually advanced for the inclusion of the freight costs is that it is part of the cost of getting the stock into the warehouse and ready for use or onward sale. Where average stockholding periods are quite long, this argument has particular validity since charging the freight to expense in the period that it is incurred could be regarded as not properly matching the costs with the revenues which is a cardinal principle of conventional accounting. This so-called 'matching' concept has a lot to answer for and has become one of the most powerful of the creative accountant's rationalisations for his black art.

The argument against including freight costs is that they are part of the ongoing cost of running the business and do not, of themselves, add any value to the stock. The concept of prudence is usually also invoked in this context by arguing that it might be optimistic to value the stocks on the basis that the company might not be able to recover this part of the cost and thus it would not be prudent to carry it forward in the balance sheet. It is ironic that, although the prudence concept and the matching concept produce different answers to this problem (and to many other accounting problems), they are both major planks of conventional accounting theory. The prudence concept is supposed to prevail when they conflict, at least according to SSAP 2, although the creative accountant will only remember this when it suits him. In short, both methods are allowed and both are widely practised. The choice of method will often depend on the result that is required and whichever is chosen will always find the support of a convincing argument.

Warehousing and handling costs
Much the same range of arguments can be advanced for the inclusion or exclusion of warehousing and handling costs. While the purist prudent accountant could argue that the cost of maintaining warehouses, stores and similar facilities is a general overhead which should be charged directly against profit, the creative accountant will argue that stock cannot look after itself and that value is added, or at least maintained, by proper storage and handling. It's a rather specious argument but it is sometimes effective, particularly when companies are producing for stock during a period of slack demand. In such circumstances, the creative accountant will often be looking for opportunities to carry forward costs in the balance sheet that he does not have to charge against profit until the good times return. If they ever do.

Overheads
Where a company produces for stock as well as buying in stock for resale, a whole new area of creative stock accounting is opened up

since there are then several additional categories of costs that can be included or excluded as necessary.

The first category of these is *labour costs*. It is generally agreed that direct labour costs should be included in the valuation. These costs are directly related to the output of the various productive processes and each unit of output can be thought of as containing so many units of labour. This approach is becoming more difficult to visualise, however, as manufacturing processes change and labour becomes less of a variable cost and more of a fixed overhead. If labour costs do not vary directly with the level of output, the inclusion of labour costs in stock valuation becomes much more of an arbitrary apportionment process and less of a logical allocation process. The distinction between apportionment and allocation is important, particularly to the creative accountant since, once the direct relationship between the incurring of a cost and the production of output is removed, it becomes easier to justify the inclusion in the stock valuation of all sorts of other costs.

Thus the door is open for the inclusion of *indirect labour costs* and the other payroll-related costs that go with them. It is now quite common for general maintenance wages, plant supervision costs and the cost of engineering staff to feature in stock valuations. The advantage of this flexibility to the creative accountant is not only that he can largely make the rules up as he goes along, but also that he can make subtle changes to what he includes and what he excludes and, therefore, massage the stock numbers without drawing too much attention to what he is doing. So often in creative accounting it is this ability to move the goal posts, inch by inch, that makes it so difficult to detect.

Once the creative accountant has included indirect costs in the stock valuation he will often go on to include the remaining categories of overheads. Overheads have two main characteristics. The first is that they are incurred in order to provide the whole production and administrative set-up of the company, including sales, distribution and general management. The second, which follows from the first, is that they usually vary with time and not with the level of production. Generally, only a limited proportion of overhead, known as *production overhead*, varies with output and it is only this element that convention and accounting standards allow to be included in stock values. In practice, however, the distinction between production overhead and general overhead is very difficult to spot and this fact will often be exploited by the creative accountant.

One common trick which can have the effect of changing the amount of overhead in the stock valuation relates to changes in the way different types of cost are allocated to different types of overhead. This will often follow from changes in the organisation of a firm, such as moving the warehousing function or, more subtly, parts of it from the distribution department to the production department. Only the auditors are really in a position to challenge this but they may not do so, even if they spot what is going on. The company will probably not volunteer any details of what they would claim is a minor administrative matter or an immaterial change in accounting policy. The claim that individual changes of this sort are not themselves material is a screen behind which many creative accountants are able to hide and much that is material in aggregate may be manipulated. The reader of the accounts has practically no hope of knowing what is going on or what the financial effects might be.

Even where this sort of trickery is not being practised, the rules about the inclusion of overheads allow, in practice, for a good deal of flexibility. As mentioned earlier, production overhead will usually vary with time. In any particular accounting period—usually a year for external financial reporting purposes—the production volume could vary considerably depending on demand and stockholding capacity. The amount of production overhead to be apportioned to each unit of the stock at the end of the period could, therefore, vary considerably from one period to the next. Where, for example, the production volume in one year was unusually low, either due to poor sales or because of a policy of running down stock levels, the amount of production overhead, which would probably be about the same amount as it would be in a normal year, would be allocated over fewer units. As a cost per unit it would thus be much higher than usual.

The accounting standard on this subject, SSAP 9, recognises this problem and provides that the amount of production overhead to be included in the year-end stock should be based on the normal level of production. A fine sentiment, but one that still allows for plenty of manipulation, particularly by the company whose production volumes genuinely vary from year to year. Design capacity or minimum profitable operating capacity could be argued to represent normal operating capacity but such figures will never be precise and can only help to avoid the most blatant abuses. What actually constitutes normal operating capacity remains a subjective assessment and the company concerned is able to take the initiative on this. The scrupulous accountant—and there are a lot of them about, in spite of the impression that this book may have given—will wish to ensure that these rules are not bent and that stock values are not manipulated. However, the reader of accounts needs to be warned that he relies on the integrity of the accountant and the quick wits of the auditor in this area, as in many others.

Volume effects

Another way of manipulating stock values is simply to manage the volume. Even when all the rules about the inclusion of overheads have been followed scrupulously in both spirit and letter, a deliberate increase in the stock level at the end of the period can have the effect of carrying forward a larger amount of overhead than in the previous year. Remember that the production overhead will mostly be incurred anyway, so carrying some forward in the stock value rather than charging it to the profit and loss account can represent a handy profit boost.

This effect may, of course, not have been intended when the decision to increase the stock holding level was taken, and it may come as something of a surprise to the accountant at the end of the year. It is amazing how many creative accounting techniques are discovered by accident. The difference between the creative accountant and his more scrupulous colleague is that the former will gladly add such discoveries to his bag of tricks, whereas the latter will studiously correct the effect of such anomalies or highlight them where they cannot be reversed.

It is, of course, true that a company cannot make a real profit merely by producing goods for stock, nor can it hide profit by running down stock levels. However, the accounting system may well have the effect of advancing or retarding the recognition of profit in the profit and loss account which has the appearance of creating or hiding profit in the short run. Sometimes, well-informed readers will know enough about the company's accounting system to know about this effect and the extent to which it can affect the reported results but many, if not most, analysts are not accountants. Indeed, many pride themselves on not knowing the ins and outs of bookkeeping practice and it is often this lack of concern with the boring technical minutiae that allows creative accounting to gain such a hold over the books.

Debtors

We have seen how the application of some imagination can produce considerable opportunities for manipulating the balance sheet value of stock and shall now go on to see what scope there is in the debtors section of the current assets. The reader might be tempted to think that it is not really possible to fiddle the debtors figure. The opportunities are, indeed, more limited but there is still some leeway for the creative accountant to produce the debtors figure that he wants in the accounts.

What makes it more difficult is that debtors are fundamentally different from stock although both are current assets. Stock is an accounting artifice in that it does not really exist in money terms, ie it cannot really be counted in money terms. Stock exists in physical terms, ie there are so many units of it or so much volume of it, but the money amount attributed to it in the balance sheet is the result of an accounting process. It is this accounting process that gives rise to the opportunities for creative accounting.

Debtors, on the other hand, exist only in money terms. They represent the next stage in the process of what is known as the cash-to-cash cycle. Companies spend cash on wages, materials and overheads and use these inputs to create stocks of finished products. When they sell these to customers they turn into debtors, ie amounts of money that are owed to the company. And when they pay up, the debtors turn back into cash again.

Like other current assets, debtors represent money tied up which the company cannot use. Although it is not usually practicable to eliminate debtors altogether unless a company's customers can be persuaded to pay in cash, the management of debtors is an important part of financial management. And what is usually meant by the management of debtors is the minimisation of the total amount owing at any one time. Unfortunately, debtor management has also become an important part of creative accounting.

Bad debt provision
The most common method of manipulating the total debtors figure is by adjusting the provision for bad debts. This unpleasant sounding item is intended to reflect that, even in the best-run

businesses, some customers will be unable to pay for the goods and services with which they have been provided. This may be because they have gone bust or perhaps because they are temporarily short of funds. Some do not pay because they dispute that the goods have been received or there is some argument about their quality. The sad truth is that such problems are inevitable although most companies take steps to ensure that bad debts are kept to a minimum by vetting credit customers in advance and setting strict credit limits.

The longer an invoice remains unpaid, whatever the reason, the less likely it is that it will ever be paid. When it becomes obvious that a particular invoice is not going to be paid the company that is owed the money will write it off against profit. This is called a specific bad debt provision because it relates to a particular debt that has gone bad. At the end of each accounting period, the accountant will have to make an estimate of how much of the total amount that he has in his books as debtors will turn out to be bad. He will make this estimate partly by looking at the bad debt experience of previous years and partly by analysing the year-end balance by the age of the debts.

While the many invoices unpaid by their due dates may just reflect some customers taking more credit than they are entitled to, they may also be an indication that some of the debts will not be paid at all. The usual procedure for calculating what is known as the general provision for bad debts is to divide the year-end balance into age bands and to apply to each band a percentage which represents the company's experience of actual bad debts. The sum of these amounts comprises the total general bad debt provision which is deducted from the figure for debtors in the balance sheet. The difference between this year's general provision and last year's is charged to the profit and loss account.

It can be seen that, while this process seems to be founded on logic and sound statistical technique, it is highly susceptible to being massaged by the creatively inclined. It is inevitably based on judgement and experience as well as on externally verifiable facts.

The attraction of the bad debt provision to the creative accountant is that it affects both the balance sheet and the profit and loss account directly and can be changed from year to year. In fact, it is to be expected that it will change from year to year as circumstances change. So, in a year when the debtors figure needs a little boost, it can be reduced and when there is scope for reducing the debtors, it can be jacked up a little. It can also be used, of course, to manipulate the profit for the year.

The adjustment process does not have to take place all in one year. If, for example, the opportunity had been taken to bump up the provision in a particular year, perhaps because the profits were a bit on the high side, it can be let out gradually over the following few years. As will be the case with many other items in the accounts, the creative accountant will probably know what the correct figure should be and will be able to calculate how much slack he has to play with by comparing the 'true' figure with the figure in the accounts. If that makes it sound like a game, many finance directors will admit in private that that is exactly how they see published financial reports. In the long run, they recognise that the truth will out, but in the meantime, they see it as part of their job to manage the process of truth dissemination in what they regard as the best interests of the shareholders.

The auditors will find it very difficult to challenge the level of the general bad debt provision, particularly if the directors are able to put together a reasonable rationale. It is fairly easy to justify a small change each year in the parameters either by appealing to recent trends or by reference to expectations. For example, the directors may claim in a year of improved sales and profits that, in their view, some of the increased trade will have been achieved at the expense of poorer quality business which is riskier than usual. Thus, they will argue, although they don't know which of their customers will default on their debts, they know that some of them will and that this will be at a higher level than last year. So it will be necessary to add a little extra to the provision to allow for this.

Being prudent men also, the auditors will probably not need much convincing since they would find it embarrassing to be associated with large write-offs in subsequent years. By the same token, they will probably not feel able to protest too strongly when it becomes apparent later on that the provision was not needed and the directors suggest that it can now be reduced. And if that happens in a year when the balance sheet is in need of some repair and the profit and loss account is somewhat short of profit, who can say that it is not just coincidence? The gradual process of bad debt provision manipulation, if played carefully, can provide the creative accountant with endless hours of amusement and profit.

Other ways of massaging debtors

While the general bad debt provision is the most effective and most widely used manipulative device with regard to debtors, there are plenty of other possibilities. They are somewhat less effective because they are short-run measures, ie while they have the desired effect in one year, they have the opposite effect in the following year. Where, however, the intention is merely to smooth profit or balance sheet changes between one year and the next, they are just the ticket.

Normally, invoices are raised when the goods are delivered to the customer or the services are rendered to him. It may often be possible, however, to advance or delay the issue of invoices depending on the desired effect. *Advancing invoices* will boost the balance sheet and increase profits and delaying them will show a weaker balance sheet and lower profits. The reason for this is that the invoice amount and therefore the amounts shown in debtors will include the profit element on each sale. In addition, it may also include the recovery of costs such as delivery and packing charges which the company may charge initially to overheads and only later credit recoveries from customers.

Customers may or may not complain about being invoiced early. They probably will not so long as it is not overdone and anyway they will probably not start counting the allowed credit period until the goods are received. They may even see it as a sign of efficiency on the part of the supplier. When invoices are issued late there are likely to be equally few complaints unless it gives the customers problems in finalising their own accounts.

The auditors should notice this since they will be concerned to ensure that the company has proper internal controls over its stock control and invoicing, and a lack of synchronisation between the despatch of goods and the raising of the associated invoices could indicate weak controls. The creative accountant will usually have prepared his story well, however, and, where invoicing precedes delivery, he will no doubt claim that property in the goods had passed to the customer early and might even go to the length of marking the goods in the warehouse with the customer's name. Sometimes the goods will actually be shipped out of the warehouse early and stored somewhere else for a while to substantiate this story. The secret of getting away with this, as with so many other creative accounting techniques, is to do only a little of it and to combine it with other procedures that work in the same direction.

Softly, softly, and the auditors, who cannot check everything, may not actually notice.

When the creative accountant wishes to reduce profits by *delaying invoicing*, he will usually have less trouble with the auditors, since this has the effect of being more conservative. He may be able to claim that, in some cases, it is possible that the customers may return the goods and this sounds quite plausible when delivery upon approval is common practice in the industry concerned. How the auditor is supposed to know which sales are on approval and which are not is anyone's guess. Even where this is not a reasonable ploy, the creative accountant could reasonably justify late invoicing to customers that have, in the past, been responsible for an unusually high level of queries and returns.

The creative accountant who is really desperate to inflate debtors can sometimes do so by *increasing prepayments*. These are payments made in one year in respect of goods or services that are received or used in the following year. Examples of prepayments are rates and rentals, deposits paid against future purchases, retainers and advances paid against future charges for consultancy and other services and royalties. This tactic is not as popular as the others mentioned earlier because it involves the expenditure of cash and the overall effect on net current assets—working capital—is zero.

Cash

It is perhaps rather surprising that, while the importance of cash management is widely recognised as being one of the most vital aspects of financial management, so little information is provided in the annual accounts about the cash position of a company at the year end and how it has managed its cash during the year.

It is often said that more companies go under because of liquidity problems than due to poor profitability. Stories abound about companies, particularly growing ones, that record satisfactory profit records for several years before succumbing to a cash crisis that either destroys them or allows them to be taken over by larger companies that are cash-rich and looking for ways to invest profitably.

The ability to pay one's way is as important for companies as it is for individuals. In the end, this means having the cash available to pay the bills as they become due and, while the business world relies upon credit to a much greater extent than individuals, there comes a time when the kidding has to stop and only cash will do.

It might be thought, therefore, that cash is cash and that there would be no scope at all for manipulating this part of the balance sheet. It is true, of course, that the rules about accounting for cash are much stricter than for some other items, both in company law and in generally accepted accounting practice, but some scope still exists for presenting the situation in the best possible light.

The first area of creative cash accounting that we shall examine concerns *the timing of payments and receipts*. Many companies will wish to show that they have as much cash in the bank as possible at the year end since this will appear as a healthier position than showing large overdrafts even if the other elements of working capital are in strong surplus. Attempts can be made to ensure that as many payments that are due to the company as possible are in its hands by the year end and are banked. This may take the form of pressing debtors for payment even when the accounts are not yet overdue although this may cost a great deal in terms of the cash discounts that have to be offered. Many large companies, however, have the commercial muscle to insist on short credit periods for their customers and to ensure that these terms are strictly adhered to. As we shall see, these are often the same companies that are able to delay payment to their suppliers with impunity and, sometimes, without having to give up their cash discounts.

Where customers cannot be persuaded to pay the full amount early, they may be persuaded to make partial payments on account or to offer post-dated cheques. Banks will sometimes credit post-dated cheques when they are paid in, although the funds from these cheques will not be considered available to the bank customer until they have been presented and cleared. This is probably a little too close to false accounting for most companies, but there is no doubt that some use this ploy. The clued-up auditor will be on the look-out for it but it may be very difficult to spot. A little of this technique will often go a long way and, when combined with other efforts that work in the same direction, is a useful weapon in the armoury of the creative accountant.

On the other side of this coin is *delaying payment*. Like advancing receipts, this may be difficult to do for many companies if they do not have the power to insist. It will be even more difficult if the company has a 31 December year end, the most common, and all the other companies in the same line of business are also trying to delay payment. This might be a contributory reason for a company to choose a less conventional year end when it may be easier to effect this kind of manipulation.

Inevitably, it will be the larger and more powerful companies that will have the most success in delaying payment. The less powerful will often have to forgo valuable cash discounts if they are to keep the cash in the bank beyond the year end. This is a classic example of how too great a concern with the appearance of accounts can cause a company to make decisions that are not in the best interests of its shareholders. It throws considerable doubt on the claims made by some creative accountants in defending their practices that, by indulging in this kind of manipulation, they are protecting the interests of their shareholders. It is probably the interests of the management and not those of the shareholders that are uppermost in the minds of the accountants who window-dress their balance sheets in such a manner.

If advancing receipts and delaying payments are not practicable, or when as much of this has been done as possible, the creative accountant has to cast around for other techniques to improve the apparent cash position in the balance sheet. One of the best known of these is *borrowing* across the year end in order to improve the ratio of available cash to liabilities. The effect of this is shown in the illustration below:

	Company A	Company B
Cash	£2,000	£7,000
Trade Debtors	£4,000	£4,000
Trade Creditors	(£8,000)	(£8,000)
Loan	—	(£5,000)
Net Position	(£2,000)	(£2,000)

Company A and Company B are identical except that Company B has borrowed an additional £5000 for the purposes of window-dressing its balance sheet at the year end. Both companies have a deficit of £2000 on working capital, ie both have £2000 more of current liabilities than they have in current assets.

But now look at the relevant ratios. These are important because they are used by financial analysts to obtain a quick insight into the financial position of a company, and the creative accountant will bear this activity in mind when deciding how best to pull the wool over the eyes of the users of his accounts. Company A has, at the balance sheet date, £2000 of liquid resources and can therefore only pay £2000 of its £8000 debts. That is, it can only pay 25 per cent of its debts. Company B, on the other hand, has £7000 with which to pay its debts of £12,000, ie it can pay off 58 per cent of its debts. Thus, its liquidity position, based on its financial ratios, looks a good deal better than that of Company A. If trade debtors are taken into account, ie if it is assumed that, by the time the company has to pay its debts it will have been paid itself, then the position of Company B still looks better. It can pay 85 per cent of its debts, whereas Company A can only pay 75 per cent of its debts. Both companies still have the same shortfall on working capital but, in proportion to the amount due, Company B seems to have less of a problem. This is, of course, more apparent than real and the improvement has only been achieved by taking on more debt which is hardly likely to be a source of balance sheet strength.

This effect can be made to look even better if the netting-off of assets against liabilities, which has been reflected in the overall shortfall position, can actually be netted off in the accounts. Generally, this is forbidden by company law and has long been frowned upon by good accounting practice, and can only be done when a legal right of set-off exists and there is firm evidence that it will actually be invoked. Even then, where the effect is material, most auditors will insist on proper disclosure in the notes to the accounts. This is an area where suspicions still linger on, however, and like many areas of creative accounting it may well be that netting-off does occur and that nobody knows about it except those who do it. A certain amount of netting-off probably goes on with or without the acquiescence of the auditors and one can only speculate as to how material the amounts are.

Much of the effort put into creative accounting for cash would be less effective if the accounts provided better information about what was happening to the cash flows into and out of a company. SSAP 10, which was introduced in 1976 to remedy this deficiency, requires that companies provide a statement of source and use of funds in addition to their profit and loss accounts and balance sheets. This statement was described on page 14. The intention behind this SSAP was that it would provide an insight into cash flows and would make up for the difficulty that the readers of the other two statements would have in forming any conclusion about what had happened during the year. The profit and loss account, as explained earlier, is based on accrual accounting and does not show directly the cash flows associated with income and expenditure items. The balance sheet only shows the cash balance at the end of the year and this, as we have seen, is capable of being manipulated. The statement of source and use of funds provides a link between the profit and loss account and the balance sheet and is designed to highlight the cash flows by eliminating the accrual effects of both statements. It emphasises funds rather than being concerned with accounting profits on the one hand or accounting measures of assets and liabilities on the other.

The intention that this statement would show clearly the company's cash flows has not been fully realised. This has been partly due to the lack of interest shown in this statement by many users, even the professional ones, and partly to the inability of the Accounting Standards Committee to agree on a single format or, indeed, to be completely clear about its objectives in this area.

In such circumstances, the creative accountant, whose intention is to conceal rather than to reveal, has a relatively easy task. The general prohibition against netting-off in the profit and loss account and balance sheet does not apply to the statement of source and use of funds. Thus, inconvenient pieces of information can be tucked away. The actual definition of funds is somewhat cloudy and different companies have different interpretations: while some attempt to get as close to cash movements as they can, others combine all sources of finance regardless of how close they are to actual cash.

Many companies do not make any real effort to identify separately the different components of cash flow, and combine cash flows from operations with investing and financing cash flows, and net off investing cash flows with those from financing. The dedicated pursuer of truth can sometimes piece together the complete picture from the information contained in various parts of the annual accounts but there seem to be few such devotees. Even the commentators in the financial press often go no further than adding net income to depreciation as a measure of gross cash flow, although some do go on to deduct capital expenditure to come up with a measure of net cash flow.

In the UK, the shortcomings of the reporting of cash flows and the ability of creative accountants to conceal the true position does not yet seem to be much of an issue. Perhaps the accounting regulators have a grudging sympathy with the view, sometimes expressed by the preparers of accounts, that cash flows are too confidential to be revealed in great detail and are the business of management rather than the shareholders. This is a difficult argument to sustain in logic, but it is currently not being seriously challenged by the investing public and the financial community.

In the USA, however, there is increasing evidence of dissatisfaction with this area of financial reporting and the flexibility in the rules which allows concealment and confusion. In 1986, the Financial Accounting Standards Board, which sets accounting standards in the USA, issued an exposure draft of a proposed standard which would require separate disclosure of cash flows from operations, those from investing activities and those from financing activities. This would severely limit the opportunities for netting-off between these categories and would require considerable detailed disclosure within categories. In another part of the exposure draft, proposals are put forward for a more direct form of presentation than that which is currently most common and which, like the UK format described above, is based on the profit and loss account.

The debate on this last aspect will be most revealing since the direct presentation will be more appealing to the financial analyst, while the conventional presentation will probably appeal more to the preparers, dominated as they are by the accounting profession. And, as we have seen, the interests of the preparers may not always coincide with those of their shareholders.

The importance of the debate in the US is that what happens today in American financial reporting often happens tomorrow— or the day after—in British accounting. The precedents for this assertion are quite persuasive, so much so that one wonders whether the UK would ever have produced accounting standards for such subjects as leasing, associates and pension costs had not the Americans led the way.

Chapter 4
Liabilities

SO MUCH FOR the assets section of the balance sheet which, as we have now seen, is not always what it might appear. It may well be accurate in the purely legal sense but may not portray economic or business reality. Instead, it may represent what its preparers would like the assets to be rather than an objective and reliable portrayal of the real investments made by the management of the company on behalf of the shareholders.

The reader will perhaps be alarmed, but not surprised by now, to discover that much the same process of fudging, fiddling and downright manipulation also goes on in respect of the liabilities side of the balance sheet. And, as with the assets, it is justified in terms of judgement and the need for flexibility. This does not mean that judgement is not needed nor that flexibility is not desirable in order to show the true and fair view but it does mean that the cynical misuse of these concepts provides the creative accountant with a cover of respectability for his misdeeds.

The first distinction to be made in this connection is that some liabilities appear on the balance sheet whereas others do not. This may seem a surprising assertion to those who are familiar with company law since it would appear to be quite clear on this point. All the liabilities of a company should appear on its balance sheet. End of story. This is, indeed, the intention of the draftsmen of the law and of the relevant accounting standards and is implicit in generally accepted accounting practice. However, by a process of side-stepping the relevant definitions and adjusting the form of certain crucial transactions, both the law and accounting standards can be avoided with ease if a company is so minded.

The liabilities that are on the balance sheet

First, let us have a look at the liabilities that are actually on the balance sheet. UK accounting practice does not really have a complete and universally agreed definition of a liability although every first-year accounting student and every businessman think that they know what is meant by the word. It is the amount that the company owes to a third party and which it must pay at some time in the future. This straightforward definition, however, melts away like the snow in spring when confronted by the determined creative accountant.

The first area to look at is *current liabilities* which will principally consist of creditors and other similar obligations of the company which are due for payment within one year of the balance sheet date. Incoming invoices which relate to goods that have been received or services that have been rendered must be recorded by the company if it is to comply with the legal requirement to keep proper books of account. The law, however, does not specify at what value these liabilities should be recorded although it is probably assumed by most users of accounts that there is only one such value.

As noted earlier, discounts may be available either for early payment or as trade discounts to provide incentives for increased volumes of purchases. The actual amount of creditors shown in a balance sheet at the end of any period will obviously depend on whether the discounts that are available have been included or excluded. There is a reasonable case for deducting trade discounts since these will be obtained by the company whether or not the invoices are paid early, but cash discounts may not usually be taken unless the early payment conditions are complied with.

Best accounting practice, therefore, as noted in connection with current assets, is that cash discounts received should be treated as equivalent to investment income since they are equivalent to compensation for loss of the use of the cash. In balance sheet terms, they should be deducted from the amount shown as current liabilities if it is the intention to pay early in order to obtain them. If it is not the intention to take advantage of the cash discounts offered, either because the company cannot afford to pay early or it has a better use for the money, they should not be deducted from creditors. Trade discounts, on the other hand, should always be deducted from creditors.

It can be seen, however, that, as with current assets, considerable scope exists for using these discounts to manipulate the amounts shown in the accounts. Once again, the creative accountant will need to have a good and convincing rationale for his chosen treatment, but it should not be difficult for him to cobble together a reasonable story, based on his knowledge of the business. As in other contexts, he can gradually modify his approach over time and involve different groups of creditors to get the effect he wants.

More scope exists regarding *accruals* that are not represented by invoices and whose existence and value have to be assessed by the accountant; it is notoriously difficult for an auditor to be sure that nothing has been excluded and that nothing is included that should not be. In the same way that prepayments can be boosted artificially by deciding to pay accounts early, accruals can be made higher or lower by a policy of withholding or advancing payment. Withholding payment is clearly more difficult than advancing it, but can be done to a limited degree. With the co-operation of the supplier, however, it can represent a considerable opportunity for manipulation. When the company concerned is a large one or a major customer, considerable pressure can be exerted on the supplier to co-operate at the year end.

Pressure of this kind has become something of a *cause célèbre* among those who champion the cause of small businesses. While the issue is not really one of creative accounting and has much more to do with the cash flow effect that such pressure has on those businesses that are least able to accommodate it, it may well be that the odium that is becoming attached to this practice may make it less popular as a creative accounting tool. Where a company is determined to do it, whether driven by the presentational aspects of financial reporting or by a desire to minimise working capital, it is unlikely that anything short of statutory action will persuade them to abandon such tactics.

Timing

The recognition of liabilities in the accounts can often depend critically on timing. The creative accountant who wants to reduce the liabilities at the year end can sometimes arrange for the delivery of goods to be delayed until after the year end so that the liability to pay for them will not have been incurred until the following year. Conversely, the advancement of delivery could be arranged so as to increase an otherwise unusually low creditors figure. This may be particularly important for companies that receive their supplies in large, discrete lumps rather than as a continuous stream throughout the year. Given the number of opportunities that exist for manipulating the various items in the balance sheet across the year end, it is amazing that people take as much notice of it as they do.

Quite often, substantial accruals have to be made on the basis of imperfect knowledge and incomplete information. The classic example occurs in the accounts of insurance companies which have to assess the amount of claims that have been incurred, ie in respect of losses and damage that have occurred by the year end but which have not yet been reported. Most industrial and commercial companies do not have an estimation problem on quite this scale but do have to deal with material estimation problems in connection with accruals.

These can vary from relatively small items such as the unbilled telephone calls outstanding at the end of a period to major items such as the amounts due on large-scale construction contracts. All of these accruals call for estimation skills and, while the honest accountant will approach the task fairly and impartially, the creative accountant will have one eye on reality and one on the result that he would like to be able to produce. As with many aspects of creative accounting, whatever effect is achieved in one year will operate in the reverse manner in the following year. This effect, of course, may be just what the creative accountant wants and, even if it is not, he will often have some other tricks up his sleeve for use in the following year.

The blind eye approach

Companies may often be reluctant to recognise certain liabilities at all. When these relate to possible legal or commercial claims the creative accountant's brief may be to provide a rationale why the liability need not be shown in the company's accounts and, if possible, whether any reference to it elsewhere can be avoided. The commercial imperatives in such circumstances may seem to be very compelling, but such practice will often be uncomfortably close to false accounting which is a criminal offence under the Companies Acts. The basic accounting concept of prudence, which we have encountered before, and which is now enshrined in company law, requires that all known losses and liabilities be provided for.

Those companies that wish to avoid the full rigour of this require-ment will usually adopt the so-called 'blind eye' approach and insist that, while the future may contain all manner of nasty surprises, they are not aware of any that require a provision to be made in the current year's accounts. This attitude may be maintained in spite of impending legal proceedings which all but the most optimistic of statisticians would regard as having a finite chance of produc-ing a liability. While putting this amount on the balance sheet — or even in the notes to the accounts — may possibly prejudice the out-come of those proceedings by appearing to admit the existence of a valid claim, its omission, if material, will seriously undermine the usefulness of the other information contained in those accounts. Even the inclusion of a note under the contingent liabilities head-ing may not be sufficient warning to the shareholders of the size and nature of the claim.

At the other extreme, some companies may be quite keen to recognise as many liabilities as possible in one particular year, either as an income-smoothing device or in order to clear the decks for an outbreak of creatively inspired profit improvement. This tactic often coincides with the arrival of a new chief executive or follows a take-over. Opportunities for this manoeuvre are manifold and difficult to challenge as it is usually characterised as that admirable accounting concept — prudence. Examples of this ploy are the setting up of a provision for product warranties or taking a pessimistic view of taxation liabilities. More will be said on these matters when discussing the techniques for massaging the income and the tax charge in Chapters 5 and 8.

Long-term liabilities

Let's move on now to the area of long-term liabilities, which are those that are not due to be paid until more than one year after the balance sheet date. The financial analysts who examine the finan-cial statements of public companies are well known for taking a short-term view of companies' prospects. This is often restricted to attempting to estimate profits for the current and the following year. Their interest in a company's financial position is as short-sighted as their interest in its financial performance and they will often effectively discount any liabilities that are seen to mature far into the future.

The requirements of company law in connection with long-term liabilities are that they should be analysed into the time periods when they become due for payment. Thus, it is probably in the interests of a company to show that as many of its debts as possible will become due for settlement as far into the future as possible. Manipulation will not, of course, be possible for those loans and other liabilities that have fixed maturity dates, even when firm arrangements exist for re-financing them, since the auditors will insist on the application of the strict letter of the law.

More scope exists, however, where loans are of indeterminate duration, even if the actual terms of the arrangement provide for repayment on demand, if the practice has been to roll them over. This sort of arrangement may be difficult to obtain in the usual financial markets but may be much more common between companies in the same group. Somewhat incongruously, the creative accountant may be able to construct a 'substance over form' argument—an argument that is usually used against him—to defend treating such loans as long term on the ground that the process of rolling over will continue indefinitely into the future. Some auditors may accept this argument, but it creates considerable dangers for the creditors of such a company who may find that what they considered to be long-term financial support from the parent company of a subsidiary suddenly withdrawn with disastrous results for the solvency of the subsidiary.

Documented long-term loans are fairly difficult to disguise even if there is some scope for fibbing about when they are going to mature. As for their amount, it might seem that there would not be any argument, but even this is not quite as clear-cut as it might seem. A particular case in point occurs in relation to *deeply discounted* or *zero coupon bonds*. These are loans made to companies by investors on which no interest or a very low rate of interest is paid. To compensate for this, the bonds are issued at a large discount to their face value, which is the amount that the company will have to pay to redeem them at some future point in time.

For example, a company may issue a bond with a face value of £100 which is the amount that it promises to repay in ten years' time. No interest is payable on the bond during this ten-year period. Assuming that the current interest rate payable on bonds of a similar maturity and risk is 12 per cent, the company will be able to sell the bond for about £32. The accounting question is: should the liability in relation to this bond be recorded at the amount of £32, the amount received, and increased by 12 per cent each year as the bond increases in value, or should the liability be recorded as £100 and the difference of £68 be recorded as a prepayment of interest to be amortised over the period of the bond? It amounts to the same thing in the end but, depending on the presentation, the financial structure of the company looks quite different.

The creative accountant might prefer one presentation to the other on purely cosmetic grounds—by definition, he will not be interested in presenting a true and fair view—or because, for example, recording the liability at £100 might infringe the company's borrowing covenants. Whenever an accounting treatment is chosen on grounds other than a genuine desire to show the transaction concerned in an impartial, neutral manner, then creative accounting is at work.

While the case of a zero coupon bond may seem to be a reasonably straightforward example, particularly if proper disclosure is provided, the creative accountant may become very interested in other aspects of his company's long-term financing arrangements, not as an aspect of financial management *per se*, but as a vehicle for misrepresentation and standards avoidance. If, for instance, the company has a long-term debt which had been issued many years ago at a fixed interest rate and this rate is materially lower than current interest rates, the market value of this loan will be considerably lower than its face value. These market values may be easily observable if the loans are traded on the Stock Exchange or they may be inferred from the difference in the interest rates.

This difference in values might suggest to the creative accountant that he should revalue these loans in the balance sheet to bring them into line with their market values. This action would seem to have the support of finance theory and correspond to economic reality. In addition, he could argue that he could obtain the same result as revaluing downward if he were to buy back the loans on the market. From an accounting point of view, the difficulty with this process is that the balance sheet is not intended to be a statement of values, at least not under the usual, historical cost, convention. Generally, assets and liabilities are not constantly revalued to reflect changes in their current values although, as we have seen, this is sometimes done for certain fixed assets.

The auditors would probably have some considerable difficulty arguing against the creative accountant. The logic might be even more compelling if the assets that were financed by the loan have been revalued. Even without this asset-liability connection, and in spite of it being an unusual accounting treatment, the auditors might be forced to agree to it and might have to be satisfied with insisting on full disclosure in the notes, at which point the creative accountant congratulates himself on another victory. Not all presentations of this type, which are now less rare than they used to be, are driven by the desire to massage the balance sheet. The difference between the honest accountant and his creative counterpart is that the latter will only adopt this technique when it suits him and drop it when it does not yield the desired result.

Off-balance sheet liabilities

As far as liabilities are concerned, the height of creativity is achieved when they do not appear on the balance sheet at all. This is not to suggest that liabilities are nasty things that accountants wish to avoid at all costs, but many boards of directors do seem to feel happier if the financial obligations of their companies are tucked discreetly out of sight where they cannot be a source of embarrassment to them. In truth, of course, liabilities are neither good nor bad, but simply represent sources of finance that have been provided by banks, debenture holders and other creditors in order to sustain the business.

Much of the concern to keep financing off the balance sheet has to do with what is known as the debt capacity of the company. There is a general feeling that any company has an ideal financial structure, an optimum balance between the finance provided by the shareholders and that provided by lenders. Since lenders require regular payments of interest and generally expect the loan to be repaid at some fixed or determinable point in the future, a company that borrows money exposes its shareholders to financial risk. This means that, in years when profits are relatively low, there may not be enough to pay a dividend as well as interest on the loans. This means that the amount left over for the shareholders will be more volatile than the pre-interest profits, since interest has to be paid before any dividend can be declared. In an extreme case, if the company is not able to pay the interest on loans at the due date or cannot repay the principal when due, the creditors can effectively take the company away from the shareholders.

Loan finance, on the other hand, has a number of advantages. First, interest payments, unlike dividends, are allowable for tax purposes, and loans are, therefore, a cheaper form of finance than equity. Second, interest payments are relatively stable and easily forecast—when profits boom, the lenders receive only their interest payments and the balance of the profit goes to the shareholders. This is the reverse of the financial risk described above.

It is this idea of financial risk that has given rise to the concept of an ideal capital structure. A certain amount of loan capital is seen as a good idea in view of the tax deductibility of the interest. Too much borrowing, on the other hand, puts the company at risk of default should the profits fall below the level at which the interest can be paid. Incidentally, many finance theorists do not believe, except in extreme circumstances, that financial structure can affect the value of companies and that there is an ideal ratio of loans to equity, but the idea is intuitively appealing. What is more important for the practical businessman is that the financial markets and the business community seem to believe it.

If there is a limit beyond which it is not safe for a company to take on additional debt, then it is something that should show up clearly in its accounts. But some boards of directors do not like being told how to run their businesses and what is proper and appropriate and will take the necessary steps to ensure that a considerable proportion of their company's debts are 'off the balance sheet'. Enter the creative accountant, sharpened pencil at the ready.

Leasing

The favourite off-balance sheet financing trick used to be leasing. Accounting standards in many countries draw a distinction between operating leases and finance leases; *operating leases* are the common-or-garden rental agreements known to corporate and individual renter alike. Under an operating lease, the lessee pays a monthly or annual rent for the use of an asset. This asset could be a photocopying machine, a video recorder, a piece of construction plant, a machine tool or an office building.

The asset remains the property of the lessor, ie the person to whom the rental is paid, in both a legal and an operational sense. If it goes wrong or breaks down, it is the lessor who has to repair or replace it, and when the lessee no longer needs it he can return it to the lessor. Subject to any conditions in the lease about the need to give proper notice, the lessee does not have to pay any further rentals once he has returned the asset in good condition.

While operating leases have some financial advantages, their main advantage to the lessee is that he does not have to take on the risks of owning the asset. This may be particularly useful if he only wants to use it for a short while or if his need for it is intermittent. *Finance leases*, on the other hand, are essentially financing arrangements disguised as rental arrangements. Although under a finance lease the lessor remains the legal owner of the asset during the period of the lease, in practice, the terms of the lease transfer the risks and rewards of ownership to the lessee. It is he who has to insure it, and repair it if it breaks down, and if he gets fed up with it or no longer has any use for it, he cannot simply cancel the lease, return the asset and stop the payments.

A finance lease usually continues in existence for most, if not all, of the economic life of the asset concerned. The rental payments paid by the lessee do not, therefore, represent charges for the use of the asset but instalments of the purchase price of the asset plus interest on the capital tied up by the lessor during the period of the lease.

Until the introduction of SSAP 21 in the UK, neither the asset nor the liability to pay the rental for many years into the future were shown on the balance sheets of lessees. Leasing, although equivalent to purchasing an asset with borrowed money, did not show up in the financial statements at all except for the rental payments themselves and then only if they were material—which, mysteriously, they never seemed to be. So while the company used the asset to produce the reported profit, its existence was not indicated in the accounts nor was the liability to pay the rentals for many years into the future.

It has been argued that, since both the asset and the liability were off the balance sheet, the net position was correctly shown and that there was therefore nothing wrong with this form of accounting. Closer examination of this argument shows that it is specious and, if taken to its logical conclusion, would have the assets and the liabilities in the balance sheet cancel each other out, leaving only the equity to be shown. The main point is that the lessee under a finance lease takes the full risk that the asset will become worthless to him, either by breaking down irreparably or through technological obsolescence, whereas he continues to be liable to pay the rentals until the end of the lease period.

The introduction of SSAP 21 has gone a long way to eliminate the off-balance sheet advantages of leasing and now the leased assets and the corresponding liabilities show up on many balance sheets. Ironically, the tax advantage of leasing which was equally responsible for its popularity as were the presentational possibilities, disappeared at about the same time as SSAP 21 became effective.

SSAP 21 has not eliminated off-balance sheet leasing entirely, however, and those creative accountants who wished to continue to hide the effect of this particular form of financing have found ways round the standard. Aided and abetted by friendly finance companies—some of which have been bold enough to advertise that they can assist clients in avoiding SSAP 21—they have been able to structure what are essentially finance leases as though they were operating leases. In the end, only auditors or shareholders can put a stop to this and, again, one can only guess at the extent to which SSAP 21 is honoured more in the breach than in the observance.

Phoney purchase schemes

A number of other off-balance sheet finance deals which have much the same kind of effect as leasing are possible. By these means, both an asset and its financing are excluded from the balance sheet. It is usually the exclusion of the liability that drives these arrangements and it is only double-entry bookkeeping that stops the creative accountant excluding the liability while including the asset! Perhaps one day he will find a way of doing that.

One well-known ploy is the *stock purchase scheme*. This involves a finance company or a bank arranging to purchase some of a company's stock or work in progress. The purchase is not genuine, of course, since the bank obtains, at the same time, an option to require the company to repurchase the stock at a particular time in the future at a price which represents the original purchase price plus an amount which represents interest on the funds tied up by the bank during its period of 'ownershsip'.

The effect on the company's accounts during this period is that stock is replaced by cash. The obligation to repurchase the stock is not recognised as a liability; indeed, the wording of the arrangement will probably ensure that it will not be. The balance sheet and the profit and loss account will look as though a genuine sale has taken place and the only trace of this arrangement will be a note about financial commitments hidden away somewhere at the back of the accounts. This arrangement is useful not only to the company that is trying to smarten up its balance sheet, but also to one whose sales are a bit on the low side one year and which would, but for this manoeuvre, look somewhat overstocked at the end of the year.

Arrangements such as these are short term, and when they unwind in the following period, the stock will come back on to the balance sheet and the outflow of cash to the bank will need to be refinanced. Another replacement arrangement may have to be put in place and, indeed, a whole series of these phoney transactions may be arranged on a rolling basis. The effective interest rate will probably be much higher than on a conventional loan due to all the extra administrative work involved on the part of the bank, but the creative accountant may be prepared to pay a little extra to have the balance sheet look good.

He may only need this arrangement at the year end to window-dress the balance sheet so that it can withstand public scrutiny, and so he may well finance the outflow during the year with ordinary loans which do not appear on any published balance sheets. Many companies do not publish balance sheets during the year, only summarised profit and loss accounts, so this little ploy can go on for ever away from the prying eyes of the shareholders and the nosy analysts.

Phoney purchase schemes can be operated in connection with any of the assets of a company, although stock is the most common vehicle. Other possibilities are *long-term work in progress and property*. Many companies that undertake long-term contracts, particularly in the construction industry, find that financing these contracts is a problem. Most ordinary lending arrangements from banks and finance companies contain restrictions which the borrower may find constraining and irksome and which might cause the shareholders to grumble if they were to appear on the balance sheet.

A solution to both problems is to 'sell' the work in progress to a bank or other financial institution. The cash received will replace the work in progress or can be used to reduce any existing borrowings, and a balance sheet that was previously clogged up with work in progress on one side and borrowings on the other, suddenly looks a lot cleaner.

At present, few companies put the value of work in progress of this sort through the sales or turnover line of the profit and loss account. For those that do, it may be possible to spot that this manoeuvre has been used since the auditors may insist on some disclosure if it is material. Where work in progress is just netted off against progress payments or is not recognised at all in the profit and loss account until finally completed, spotting this kind of deal is almost impossible.

Sale and repurchase agreements are more difficult to operate as off-balance sheet financing when fixed assets are used because of the company law requirement that capital commitments are disclosed, and an arrangement to repurchase a fixed asset could count as a capital commitment. This disclosure only occurs in the notes to the accounts, however, and usually very little detail is provided. And, while the Accounting Standards Committee and others ritually intone the conventional wisdom that the notes are an integral part of the accounts and must be taken seriously, they are little used in practice. Even professional users of accounts such as financial analysts seem to take little notice of what is in the notes and one hardly ever sees a reference to capital commitments in stockbrokers' reports. By the time any real notice is taken of this information the damage has been done and off-balance sheet finance may often only become apparent when a company begins to go under.

It is this that makes off-balance sheet finance such a dangerous practice and it has been called the corporate equivalent of alcoholism or drug dependence in an individual. The appearance of health and normality can, with a considerable effort, be maintained for quite a long time, but when the truth finally breaks through the sufferer may be so far gone that recovery is no longer possible.

The hidden subsidiary
So far, this section on off-balance sheet financing has concentrated on the measures that the creative accountant can take to keep borrowings out of the accounts of an individual company. For many companies, however, the balance sheet that receives most attention is the consolidated balance sheet of the group headed by the company as parent. This balance sheet, which is prepared as though the parent and all its subsidiaries were a single entity, contains all the assets and liabilities of all the group companies. A priority for the creative accountant who is operating off-balance sheet finance in a group of companies is to keep the borrowings off the consolidated balance sheet.

This can be achieved by what is known variously as the hidden subsidiary or the controlled non-subsidiary. It consists essentially of channelling borrowings into a company that is effectively controlled by the parent company of a group, but which is not technically a subsidiary. Since the controlled company is not a subsidiary, its balance sheet does not have to be consolidated and its borrowings do not appear in the group accounts. The hidden subsidiary is only hidden from the point of view of the users of the accounts of the parent and will, of course, have to publish its own accounts, showing its borrowings. The connection between the parent and the hidden subsidiary will not be easy to spot, however, and its existence may never be known to the shareholders in the parent. Thus, this borrowing remains at a discreet distance from the group for whose benefit it has been raised.

The secret lies in ensuring that the hidden subsidiary is set up in such a way that legally it is not a subsidiary of the company that controls it. Under current company law, a company is a subsidiary of another if that other company owns a majority of its equity capital or is able to control the composition of its board of directors. So, in order to keep the unwelcome borrowings off the consolidated balance sheet, the creative accountant and his equally creative legal colleagues will have to ensure that neither condition is met.

The easiest and most popular way of dealing with the first condition is to set up the share capital of the hidden subsidiary as consisting of two separate classes, say ordinary shares and 'A' shares, and equal numbers of each class of shares are issued. The difference between the two classes of shares is that the ordinary shares carry a vote and the 'A' shares do not. In addition the 'A' shares carry an entitlement to a dividend which is based on current interest rates and will probably vary as interest rates vary. The 'A' shares are then issued to the controlling company's friendly banker. The ordinary shares, which carry the right to the residual profit as well as carrying a vote, are issued to the controlling company.

Thus, the controlling company has complete control over the hidden subsidiary, but only owns half its equity capital. The bank, or other financial institution, has invested in the hidden subsidiary nominally by subscribing for shares but, in reality, it has the same interest in its fortunes as it would had it made it a normal loan since the shares carry no voting power and produce a dividend income exactly equal to the interest that would be earned on a loan. So that the bank may get its money back at some time in the future, the 'A' shares may have to be made redeemable, but this may not be necessary if the bank has some other security from the controlling company.

Even though the 'parent' controls the hidden subsidiary and is the only real shareholder in that it alone has the residual interest in the hidden subsidiary's income because the law regards all equity capital as equivalent, the hidden subsidiary is, technically, not a subsidiary. The inequality in voting power and the difference in dividend entitlement do not enter into consideration nor does the fact that the friendly bank is effectively acting not as a shareholder, but as a lender.

To make the hidden subsidiary's position completely watertight, the composition of the board of directors has to be considered. This is important because it is the board that will make the operating decisions of the hidden subsidiary. The voting power of the shares can only be used in general meetings of the company and is a more cumbersome process of deciding on company policy than the day-to-day decision-making process of the board. Hence the legal requirement that if one company controls the composition of the board of another, it must consolidate that other.

In order that the controlling company may control the actions of the board of the hidden subsidiary without controlling its composition, the creative accounting and legal team will usually advise that, while each shareholder may nominate the same number of directors, those nominated by the controlling company shall have ten times as many votes as those nominated by the bank. Thus, the controlling company does not control the composition of the board since it can only nominate half its members but it is able to control its decisions.

A further variation on this theme is that each board member has the same number of votes but that those appointed by the bank make an arrangement not to vote at board meetings, leaving the way clear for the controlling company's nominees to control the operating decisions. This carries the slight risk for the controlling company that the directors nominated by the bank might assert their rights and vote in a way that is contrary to the interests of the controlling company. Such an eventuality is rather unlikely, however, since the bank may have been the prime mover in setting up the arrangement and would not normally be prepared to upset its client by acting in this way. In practice, therefore, the cosy unanimity of the board is not likely to be disturbed.

Having set up the hidden subsidiary, the controlling company may now arrange for it to take on borrowings which will never have to appear in the consolidated balance sheet although the funds can be used for the purposes of the group. Care must be taken as to how these funds are actually used since they cannot be loaned to a group company. If this were to occur, the loan would go into the group company's balance sheet and thence into the consolidated balance sheet and the whole point of the charade will have been lost. However, the funds can be used to buy assets that are then hired to a group company under an operating lease—probably at a very low rental or simply to finance group assets which are sold to the hidden subsidiary and also disappear from the consolidated balance sheet. What to do with the money is a small problem compared to the care and attention that will have been given to the problem of keeping its existence away from the prying eyes of the accounts-reading public.

This form of off-balance sheet finance is particularly worrying because it is so hard to detect. In recent years, more than one company which had got into financial difficulties was forced to reveal enormous off-balance sheet financing arrangements which made their rescue all the more difficult. Even the most sharp-eyed analyst or lending officer will not usually be able to spot the scale or existence of this type of off-balance sheet financing. Even worse, the management of the controlling company may come to believe that the accounts that it presents to the outside world are actually true and fair and may act in ignorance of the real situation and the real pressures that could be building up within the group. In the country of the blind, the one-eyed man may be king, but the leader who is also blind but thinks that he can see is a grave danger to society.

What can be done about it?

Off-balance sheet financing in all its forms, but particularly the hidden subsidiary manoeuvre, is under attack from two directions—the ASC and company law are both moving in on it. The ASC is rightly concerned that the existence of off-balance sheet financing on a major scale is a real and serious threat to the integrity of financial reporting and to the role of the ASC in regulating it. Moves were under way at the time of writing to develop means of dealing with this threat. The basis of this approach is likely to be an agreed definition of assets and liabilities that will not allow the technical structure of a transaction to obscure the economic reality that underlies it nor prevent its recognition in financial statements.

This may be supported by the well-established principle of substance over form, although there are those in the legal profession who doubt that this concept is operable in practice. This principle states that financial statements should reflect the economic and commercial reality of a transaction rather than only its legal form. This principle, in spite of legal doubts, has already had some notable successes, particularly as regards accounting for leases, and the whole structure of consolidated accounts is based on the substance of the group rather than its existence as a separate legal entity. Its application in individual cases is as difficult as its general objective is clear, since it is often a matter of fine judgement as to what the economic and commercial realities are, whereas the legal form can usually be determined relatively easily.

Nevertheless, the ASC and the accounting profession seem determined to overcome this problem. It is vital that they do, since failure could undermine the very structure of financial reporting and with it much of economic substance in the UK. Such failure— or even its contemplation—is not likely to be tolerated by government which would certainly act to take the process of accounting standard setting out of the hands of the accounting profession and the business community and give it, instead, to the Civil Service. This is both an implied promise and a serious threat.

The practice of off-balance sheet financing is also under attack from European company law. The EC Seventh Company Law Directive is due to be implemented into UK company law by 1990. This Directive, which is concerned with the preparation and publication of consolidated accounts, sets out a wider definition of a subsidiary than the current UK definition. The definition in the Directive is based on control rather than ownership and would require the consolidation of an entity in which the parent had a controlling interest. This provision would catch some, if not all, of the current generation of hidden subsidiaries that are now able to slip through the rather coarse net of UK company law. It is to be hoped that this provision will be enacted into UK law in a way that ensures that it is effective in reducing, and perhaps eliminating, this particular form of off-balance sheet financing.

This does not mean, of course, that the creative accountant will just give up and go away. Shutting one door will possibly allow another to open and one can be sure that the creative accountant will soon be actively looking for ways round the new law and any changes in accounting standards that are introduced to combat this problem. In this dubious task he will no doubt be aided by an increasing and increasingly skilful band of advisers, particularly from the rapidly expanding financial services sector of the economy. The vigour and imagination of this sector is, in many ways, a valuable contribution to the general economic well-being of the country and is seen by many commentators as providing an element of hope for our post-industrial future.

Among such a dynamic and creative community there are, however, always some individuals who put their skills and energy towards ends that are not in the long-term best interests of either their clients or the community at large. It is important that they are persuaded to apply their talents to more productive activities or we run the risk of the authorities taking action that will not only abolish creative accounting but may, at the same time, irreparably damage the usefulness and credibility of financial reporting. The best way to stop creative accounting is by a general process of education and criticism and, fortunately, this seems to be under way, at least as far as off-balance sheet finance is concerned. Vigilance is necessary by both the accounting profession and the business community, together with a determination to root out what could become a dangerously malignant tumour in the body of British business.

Chapter 5
Income

SO FAR, WE have looked at how the creative accountant can massage and manipulate the balance sheet from the raw, unformed document that first emerges from the company's bookkeeping system to the final polished product that drops through the shareholder's letterbox. It is, however, not only the balance sheet that enjoys this grooming process. The profit and loss account is also sent to the creative accountant's charm school before it is presented to the world.

The creative accountant is the ultimate realist. All he is really after is a breathing space, knowing that in the long run it will all come out in the wash.

Part of this never-ending story is the process of becoming gradually better off which is known in the financial community as profitability. While academic accountants and economists agonise over what income really is and how it should best be measured, the man in the street has very little problem with income recognition. He may have a problem with the size of his income, but he has no problem recognising it. His income is the amount that he receives regularly and which he uses to pay his bills and other living expenses. If he has anything over, he saves it, and if he is a bit short he borrows or draws on his previous savings. He knows if he is getting richer or poorer without the need for accounting. He also knows—wise man—that creative accounting cannot help him to improve his standard of living. Only more money can do that.

The problem with company accounting is that it is not based only on cash but, as noted in Chapter 1, on the accruals concept. This means that the income that a company receives in a year is not the same as the net increase in the cash in its bank account over the year. Its gross income, its revenue, is the value of the goods and services that it has delivered to customers during the year. It may not have received payment for all or even any of these goods during the year although it will only count as income those items of revenue that it expects will eventually turn into cash. Much of the cash it has received during the year may relate to income earned in the previous year.

Whether or not cash has been received is not, of itself, important although it does help to determine whether real income has been earned or whether the company has just given its stock away. Income recognition reflects economic activity during the year and requires more skill than just the ability to add up the amounts on the company's paying-in slips. The application of the accruals concept needs to be tempered with prudence and with the principle that income may not be recognised in accounts until it has been realised. All very fine accounting principles these, well known to accountants and businessmen and all capable of being manipulated in the most cynical way in the pursuit of the creative accountant's own view of economic truth.

The reason that manipulation and massaging are so easy is that old accounting chestnut—judgement. It is true that no two accountants will produce exactly the same profit and loss account from the same set of transactions except in a professional examination where all the uncertainties are eliminated and all assumptions are uniform. In the real world, many uncertainties remain and the accountant must make a wide variety of assumptions about how certain situations will turn out. Will the customer pay his bill? Will the cost of materials needed to finish a job that is under way at the year end go up or down? Will customers find faults in the goods they have bought and insist on either a refund or a replacement? Are the fixed assets still worth the value at which they are stated in the balance sheet? All these assumptions and many more will have to be addressed and made explicit in order to finalise the accounts.

There is no particular cause for alarm in the realisation that different accountants will take different views regarding these assumptions, so long as they are taken honestly and are based not only on professional skill but also on professional integrity. Accounting principles can only guide the accountant as to how to deal with particular situations—they cannot make his decisions for him. All they can hope to do is to ensure that, in broadly comparable circumstances, broadly comparable results are produced.

Comparability requires that like transactions are accounted for in the same way and that different transactions are accounted for in a way that reveals their differences. Judgement is therefore essential and any regime of accounting regulation that effectively eliminates the need for judgement will do as much to harm financial reporting as one that contains no guiding principles at all.

The arbitrariness of the accounting period

The first major area that gives rise to the need for accounting judgement and where, therefore, creative accounting may creep in relates to the arbitrary nature of the accounting period. For an agricultural community, the year is a natural accounting period. By the time the harvest is in and the accounts have been settled, the contents of the farmer's barn and wallet can be known with reasonable certainty. For an individual, the year may be a less natural accounting period, but he will have little difficulty in calculating his income.

A business, on the other hand, undertakes a variety of transactions. While some of these may be very short term in nature, others may be of much longer duration. Each day, every business in the country will be embarking on the first stages of one transaction while at the same time being in the middle of another and in the final stages of a third.

The length of what is known as the cash-to-cash cycle will vary considerably between companies in different businesses and between different businesses carried on by the same company. The longer the cash-to-cash cycle, the more judgement is required in determining accounting income. For example, a retailer will probably sell the vast majority of its turnover to customers who pay immediately in cash and consume the goods fairly soon after purchase. There is little doubt for such businesses what the income figure is and, therefore, little opportunity for manipulating this figure in the accounts short of outright fraud. The accountant will know fairly soon if any of the customers have cause to return faulty goods and, with lots of relatively small transactions going through the books, the use of statistical techniques to assess likely returns will be reliable enough. There will be some, fairly minimal, scope for tweaking the statistical method of calculating the amount to be deducted for returns, but the amounts involved are unlikely to be material and the auditors will be ready to challenge anything that is.

Long-term contracts

Where companies engage in long-term contracts the outcome of which may not be known for several years, an assessment of the amount of revenue and profit that should be brought into account in any one year is much more problematical. All companies seem to like to show a steady upward trend in sales figures (we shall see more about massaging trends later) and so the creative accountant may be called upon to ensure that the sales revenue recorded under long-term contracts produces this comforting trend line.

Clearly, any accountant who has to deal with revenue recognition in connection with long-term contracts has to take a view about how much should be included in any one year and this problem is more difficult at the beginning of a contract than it is at the end when the uncertainties are much reduced. Most accountants will wish to be reasonably prudent about how much revenue is reported in each year since they will not like to have to admit later on that they had been somewhat over-optimistic in the earlier years. Judgement, however, can easily tip over into manipulation when, having done the initial sums, the creative accountant then makes additional adjustments to get the answer that he wants.

He may decide to suppress turnover in one year, perhaps because other contracts that are close to completion have produced revenue and profits that are higher than expected or because he suspects that the following year's results are not going to be as good and could use a little secret boost. To do this, he only needs to be particularly conservative about how much revenue to recognise in the first year. For example, measuring points for progress payments could be moved into the following year. This would then allow a very cautious view to be taken of the amount of revenue-earning work completed by the year end, perhaps even going as far as recognising no revenue earned beyond the previous progress payment stage.

If and when it becomes necessary to speed up the recognition of revenue when more turnover is required to improve the look of the results, the creative accountant has only to return to a more reasonable and less cautious approach. The use, at this time, of an independent quantity surveyor will add a good deal of credence to this process. The only strong evidence that this process of manipulation is not going on is the existence of an independent valuation every year. Few companies do this, of course, because it is expensive, but this means that, in practice, it is difficult to tell the manipulators from the rest. Perhaps the only sensible advice to the users of accounts of companies with a heavy involvement in long-term contracts is not to rely too much on the profit and loss account at all and concentrate on cash flow information.

Even when the valuation is undertaken by an independent valuer, the creative accountant still retains some scope for manipulating the final result. He might claim that a provision for reworking or rejection is needed and that the estimate produced by the valuer should be reduced. Alternatively, when he needs a little more revenue, he may be prepared to take a more optimistic view and reduce the level of provision, make none at all, or take something back out of the balance sheet provision that he had set up in previous years. This is very similar to the game that he can play with the bad debt provision that we encountered in Chapter 3 and it is very difficult for the auditor to argue with. It is almost impossible to spot without detailed inside knowledge of the company's business, which makes it a particularly useful weapon in the creative accountant's armoury.

Bad debt provisions revisited

The sad fact that some customers fail to pay for the goods and services with which they have been provided is not an unmitigated disaster for the creative accountant. To him, it is the silver lining that accompanies the proverbial cloud. We saw in Chapter 3 how the bad debt provision can be used to massage current assets. The articulation of the balance sheet with the profit and loss account means that it can also be used to massage the revenue picture. The setting up of a provision for bad debts and subsequent increases in that provision are usually charged to the profit and loss account as an expense. Since this treatment does not affect the sales revenue it has the effect of reducing the gross margin in percentage terms. This may be unwelcome to the creative accountant who, while being happy to reduce profit, might not want any hassle from the analysts about reducing profitability. So instead of charging the default to expenses, the creative accountant might try to treat it as a reduction in turnover, which means that the gross margin is not harmed. The effect of this is shown below:

	Before	After
Revenue	100	90
Cost of Sales	(50)	(50)
Bad Debt Write-off	(10)	—
Profit	40	40
Gross Margin	40%	44%

In the 'after' situation above, the bad debt has been treated as a reduction in the revenue as though the sale had not taken place by the ploy of issuing a credit note to cancel the original invoice issued. This may seem rather close to false accounting and illustrates that there is sometimes a fine line between creative accounting and illegal falsification of the accounts. However, it can still be done, although if the auditors spot it and it becomes too public, it can lose its effectiveness. Still, if it is done in moderation, as it probably is in countless companies, it will go unnoticed. And you can be sure that the creative accountant and his creative marketing colleagues will have a convincing story ready. The auditor will find it very difficult in such circumstances to distinguish the genuine credit note from the one designed to massage the revenue figure.

The enthusiasm of the City and other commentators for steady increases in turnover with no sudden and unexpected reversals is to blame for much of the creative accountant's passion for revenue manipulation. Even where the profit trend is satisfactory, the financial analysts in the City become decidedly nervous about a company whose revenues are somewhat erratic and, amazingly, this seems to apply even to those companies whose businesses are cyclical and for whom a smooth progression of revenue increases is actually a bit suspicious. One cannot, of course, blame the 'square mile' for the whole of creative accounting, but without this motivation to present a sanitised picture free of all nasties and surprises, one wonders how much manipulation of published financial statements would go on.

Other problems of revenue recognition

A number of industries are particularly prone to difficulties of income recognition. Of these, the extractive industries and the financial sector provide two examples which, although they are markedly different in their technology and markets, share a common problem and provide similar opportunities for massaging income.

The extractive industries include mining for metals and other minerals, and the oil and gas sector. All produce goods which are commodities and for which an active and efficient market exists. While mining and oil companies are usually large, the industries and markets that they operate in are larger still. As a result, they are not alone able to influence the prices in the market and are forced to act as price takers rather than price makers. The depth and sophistication of the markets, particularly when options and futures are available, means that these companies do not necessarily have to seek out the final consumers of their productive processes but can, if they wish, sell through dealers and brokers. In short, once they have produced, and perhaps refined, their products, they have done nearly all they need to do in order to realise their income.

Many of the companies in these industries do not recognise their income on this basis but wait until they have sold their products to a customer. There are others, however, that take the view that they have realised their income when they have produced the minerals: they overlook the normal accounting rule that income cannot be recognised until it has been realised and that it cannot be realised until it has been sold to a third party. They find this rule especially galling if they have transferred the product from one division to another at cost and cannot, under this rule, include anything for this transfer in their profit and loss account. A viable alternative, given the existence of an active and efficient market, is for one division to sell into the market and for the other to buy from the same market.

This manoeuvre is exactly what the creative accountant advises and stock is magically turned into revenue. This can be done with ease by the large integrated oil company which would normally transfer crude oil at cost—considerably lower than the market price—from its 'upstream' production division to its 'downstream' refining and marketing division. When a fillip is required to turnover or profit, this transfer goes via the market, even though this may cost something in terms of the margins required by market traders. (Occasionally, these companies can manage to have it both ways by playing the markets and making trading profits rather than having to pay a margin.) When less turnover and profit are required, the transfer is made internally.

Within the extractive industries, concern about this practice and the difficulty of spotting it has led to the argument being advanced that mining and oil companies should value their stocks at net realisable values and should recognise their profits on production rather than on sale. Interestingly, the EC Seventh Company Law Directive on consolidated accounts allows member states to permit the recognition of intra-group profits in such circumstances, although the corresponding directive on the accounts of individual companies does not provide a corresponding treatment for unrealised commodity profits. The UK government has not shown much interest in the provision of the Seventh Directive as yet, but this may be because the creative accounting opportunities afforded by the current practice are not yet well known.

Loan fees and costs

It is perhaps not surprising that the financial community which has both demanded creative accounting from companies and provided advice on how to do it should be an active participant in this game. One particular aspect where the scope for income massaging is considerable relates to the recognition of fees and costs received and incurred by banks in connection with setting up loans. Corporate finance is very big business today for the merchant banks and other financial institutions whether they finance the loans themselves or act as intermediaries for a group of lenders. In the process of setting up these loans for industrial and commercial companies, these banks will often incur large costs by way of fees and commissions and will often receive sizeable fees either from their clients or from the other finance houses on whose behalf they act.

The accounting treatment of these fees and costs varies from bank to bank and, one suspects, from time to time. They can either be recognised in full when they are received or paid, be spread over the life of the loan by way of an adjustment to the interest rate or deferred until the loan has largely matured. It can be seen that the total number of permutations and combinations of these different accounting methods provides an enormous amount of flexibility and the potential for income manipulation is considerably enhanced if different treatments are given to different elements at different times.

In the USA, the situation has become so chaotic that the Financial Accounting Standards Board has issued a technical bulletin to bring some order and comparability. Essentially, this says that all these items should be taken into income as an adjustment to the interest rate charged over the full life of the loan. In the UK, however, there is no mechanism for developing accounting standards for individual industries since the Accounting Standards Committee has decided that it can only deal with issues of fundamental importance that affect the generality of companies. It is, of course, open to a body representing the financial community to propose a non-mandatory Statement of Recommended Practice and there is some evidence that the banking industry at least is moving to tackle some of these issues. Whether a non-mandatory statement can really make much headway in an area where even mandatory standards and the intentions of the legislature can be avoided with seeming ease must be open to considerable doubt.

Revenue or capital?

Further examples of creative accounting are provided by the distinction between revenue and capital receipts or other non-recurring gains. As we shall see in Chapter 6, the idea that certain types of transaction are not typical of the year or the business and may be excluded in calculating profit—or, to be more precise, earnings per share—provides a classic creative accounting opportunity. By the same token, when non-recurring income arises, the creative accountant's eyes light up since here is another opportunity to massage the financial statements.

Turnover is supposed to represent the sales proceeds that a company has earned from carrying on its normal business with the outside world. The dividing line between normal trading and extraordinary items is often blurred when, for example, the question arises as to how the proceeds of the sale of a fixed asset or an investment should be accounted for. Some might argue that the proceeds should be shown as income with the associated book value included under costs of sale, whereas others would net off the proceeds and the book value and show only the difference under income. A further variation would net off any profit against the book values of other assets of the same type if they could all be regarded as a single portfolio, thereby deferring the recognition of the income until a later, and presumably more convenient, accounting period.

Whether the full amount of the proceeds of this type of transaction shows up in revenue is, therefore, somewhat random. If the accountant who is making the decision is of the creative persuasion, the decision will be based on what he wants the answer to be rather than what he thinks is the fairest and most realistic representation. Best practice would probably dictate that, if the proceeds are shown in revenue and the amount is material, it should be disclosed together with the profit or loss on the transaction, but the creative accountant would probably not heed such advice. If he needs to increase the revenue this year he will almost certainly put such income into the profit and loss account without any disclosure and argue that it was the normal business of the company to change its mix of investments from year to year. The strange thing is that he might well find himself arguing the opposite case in the following year if his presentational needs are then different. The most useful antidote to creative accounting is a long memory, both on the part of the auditor and the user of the accounts.

Some might argue that, in the final analysis, it does not matter how items are actually treated in financial statements so long as there is adequate disclosure. There is a danger, however, that the disclosure may become so voluminous that it would amount to 'information overload', the consequences of which are that important information becomes impossible to discern among the mass of detail. Anyway, it is generally recognised that disclosure can never make up for poor accounting, even though it is often used to justify it.

As noted earlier, the more complicated or esoteric a transaction, the easier it is to manipulate the recognition of revenue. This is more difficult when there is an accepted body of accounting practice or when the prudence concept is a dominant factor as it is in, for example, the insurance industry. However, in new and rapidly expanding sectors, the opportunities for accounting creativity expand with the invention of each new financial product.

Innovative financial instruments

A particular area of concern at present relates to the rapid expansion in the volume and complexity of financial instruments that are available not only to the banking community but to customers in the wider business world. The technology of this market is expanding fast and each week seems to bring a new permutation or a new combination of transactions. Talk of interest rate swaps, straddles, spreads and options on futures is confusing to all but the most sophisticated of the new breed of City slickers. While most of these operations and transactions have a genuine business purpose and can be accounted for properly once the true nature of the underlying transaction is understood, there is no doubt that some of the motivation behind some of the high-pressure promotion of these deals is the opportunity they present for creative accounting.

For an example of this, let us look at the futures market. For a company that holds and uses stock that is a commodity traded on a reasonably efficient market, there is little economic difference between holding physical stock and holding a long position in the futures market, since having the stock and being able to buy it in the future at a fixed price amount to the same thing. However, the accounting treatment of these two situations will usually be quite different. If the company holds the stock, it must normally value it at the lower of cost or net realisable value. If it holds a futures position, however, this is usually valued at market prices. When the market price is considerably above cost, a company holding a futures position will be able to advance the recognition of profit compared to a company that is holding physical stocks.

Increasingly, City institutions, staffed as they are by a considerable number of people who have had accountancy training or who understand the flexibility that exists in the rules, are alert to the demand for creative accounting and are able to tailor transactions so that they will have the desired accounting effect. Deals can therefore be put together, not on the basis of the underlying business reality but according to how they will look in the accounts. Finance directors are also aware of the facilities that are available in the City for massaging their accounts and may pay more attention to the cosmetic accounting effects than to whether the transactions proposed are really in the interests of their company.

Like a lot of creative accounting, this area is extremely difficult to detect in practice. The accounting policies note will usually say little or nothing about how financial transactions are accounted for—well, they wouldn't, would they? It would be a brave company that was prepared to say that its financial transactions were always accounted for strictly in accordance with their true natures and not only according to the legal forms that had been structured for them. Any finance director that made such a statement would have to hang up his creative accounting gloves and rejoin the minority that really believe that financial statements should be true, fair and impartial.

Chapter 6
Expenses

EXPENSES ARE DEDUCTED from revenue in arriving at profit. Since it is profit that is usually the prime object of the creative accountant's manipulations, massaging the expenses so that they turn out to be what he wants them to be is a major preoccupation of the creative accounting process.

Expenses are not the same thing as costs. Although all expenses *are* costs of one sort or another, an important point to remember when trying to untangle the web of creative accounting is that not all costs are expenses—unless, that is, you want them to be. As we have already seen, much of creative accounting is about managing trends and making sure that there are no unpleasant or unexpected surprises when the half-year or annual accounts are announced. So manipulating the expenses is an important part of the process of creating the cosy atmosphere of steadily increasing profits.

When the creative accountant wants to reduce the expenses figure he can defer the costs, he can capitalise them (and remember, he may or may not have to depreciate these capitalised costs), he can charge them against a provision or he can charge them directly to reserves. When he wants to find more expenses in a year, perhaps because his profit is higher than he wants it to be, or larger than it is likely to be in the following year, he can create a provision, accrue some unnecessary expenses or change the rate at which a prepaid expense is amortised or a fixed asset depreciated.

The variations are seemingly endless and, if he is clever, he will not tweak any of these little ploys so hard that it becomes obvious. A little bit of creativity here and there and—hey presto—out pops just the right profit number for his purposes. And no one, not even the auditors, can complain too much. The creative accountant will no doubt argue that the constant changes reflect the dynamic business environment in which the company is operating and that it must continually adapt if it is to survive. Moving with the times necessarily means making the odd change to accounting policies here and there, he claims, and requires that a different overall view be taken at different times. It is fine tuning, nothing more—and if the end result just happens to be that the profit is more or less what the directors had in mind... well, they are the ones who have to sign the accounts, aren't they?

The price-earnings ratio

One reason that the profit figure is so important is that it is an input to one of the City's favourite quick and dirty indicators of performance—the price-earnings ratio, or P/E. This is obtained by dividing the current share price by the earnings per share. Earnings is defined as profits after tax but excluding extraordinary items. The exclusion of extraordinary items is particularly important in this context as we shall see later.

The P/E ratio is used to compare one company with another. Usually, this comparison is limited to companies in the same sector as it is not realistic to compare companies in completely different businesses since they will experience different risk and reward patterns. The truth of this can be seen by looking at the P/E ratios in the *Financial Times*: each sector has a range of P/E ratios which is different from those in other sectors. For example, banks will usually have P/E ratios in the 5-10 range whereas companies in the stores sector will often have ratios in the twenties or thirties.

The P/E ratio is believed to reflect whether a company is over- or undervalued compared with other companies in the same line of business. Stockbrokers' analysts are in the business of trying to identify which shares are worth buying and which should be sold. Ideally, they would like to be able to find a share that is undervalued at one point in time so that they can recommend that their clients buy it and later, when it has gone up in price, to identify it as being overpriced and to advise the same clients to sell. Everyone is happy: the client makes a profit and the stockbroker picks up two lots of commission. The desire by stockbrokers to create turnover and thereby profit from the commissions generated is a worrying source of conflict of interest between stockbroker and client.

P/E ratios, of course, reflect not only the share price but the profit and many companies will have target P/E ratios or a range of P/E ratios within which they would like their shares to move. While they will not wish to see them chronically undervalued and languishing in the fourth division of the Stock Exchange, they will equally not want them to soar unwarrantedly and then collapse. Boom and bust is not a formula for pleasing the City and the institutional shareholders, so achieving and maintaining the desired P/E ratio means achieving the desired profits.

Deferred expenditure

How, then, does the creative accountant go about massaging the expenses? Let us start by assuming that he wants to reduce the expenses so as to boost profit. The first step is to find a method or a combination of them for deferring unwelcome costs into future periods. They will, of course, appear in the profit and loss account some time, unless they are deferred indefinitely, but that may be the objective. Or the creative accountant may be able to dream up another deferral and keep the ball in the air for ever.

One way of deferring expenditure is to include it in the valuation of stock, as we observed in Chapter 3. There is a whole range of justifications for doing this, usually based on the rationale that the costs have been incurred in getting the stock into the location or condition that makes it available for use or resale. Many different types of costs can be deferred in this way including transport, production and storage costs, as well as a variety of production, distribution and even administration overheads. The calculation of how much cost can go into stock allows for a considerable number of variables and a gentle massaging of some or all of them is often all it takes to move the answer in the desired direction by the desired amount.

Work in progress is another fruitful area where the deferral of costs may be possible, particularly where the company has one or more long-term contracts under way which are known to be profitable (one might ask how it is possible to know that anything is profitable with all this fiddling going on, but that is another question). In these circumstances, some costs which probably ought to be written off in the period can be included in the valuation of work in progress and carried forward. This has the effect of recognising some of the profit on the contract rather earlier than it otherwise would have been. It is notoriously difficult for the users of accounts, or even auditors, to come to different conclusions on the correct treatment of these costs from that of the management and this process can go on unnoticed almost indefinitely.

Capitalisation

Another popular method of deferring costs into the future is to capitalise them, ie to include them in the balance sheet as fixed assets. It may surprise the uninitiated reader to discover that many of the fixed assets in the balance sheet are not tangible like plant and machinery but may, instead, be intangible such as research and development expenditure, patents, trademarks and goodwill.

Almost any kind of cost can be capitalised. Ideally, it should be related to a tangible fixed cost as this helps in the process of justification. Thus, the construction by a company of its own fixed assets provides an ideal opportunity for the creative accountant who wishes to tuck away sizeable amounts of wages, materials, transport, spare parts and overheads into the fixed asset accounts, providing the profit and loss account with an 'expenses holiday' and improving the balance sheet at the same time. Many companies have a policy of capitalising interest incurred on money borrowed to finance the construction of new fixed assets. In principle, there can be no objection to this since the interest can be regarded as a legitimate part of the cost of acquiring the asset. In the hands of the creative accountant, however, this practice is clearly capable of considerable manipulation and its effect may be difficult to determine even when the company discloses that it capitalises interest.

Most companies have laid down accounting policies about what should and should not go into fixed assets but, once again, we shall see that the creative accountant does not need to break the rules in order to get his own way. It is his ability to bend the rules and interpret them to his advantage that makes the whole process of creative accounting largely invisible. For example, the accounting policy may say that only direct costs may be capitalised. In this case, the internal costing methods may have to be changed so that what was previously regarded as indirect costs become direct costs and can now be capitalised. Much of the desired effect can often be achieved by the boring, but for the creative accountant rewarding, task of coding invoices so as to ensure that as much as possible gets into the direct cost category and, therefore, into fixed assets and the safe haven of the balance sheet.

The sharp-eyed auditor will sometimes be able to spot a change in the pattern of direct and indirect allocations, particularly when a major construction project is under way. If he feels brave enough, he may be able to challenge the propriety of this. In practice, of course, few audits delve into this level of detail and the amounts involved in this particular manipulation may not be material enough for the auditor to become unduly concerned.

Research and development

Another useful deferral opportunity concerns research and development expenditure. This is apparently regulated by an accounting standard—SSAP 13—but, in practice, considerable scope still exists for using the R and D accounts to tuck away unwanted expenses. The secret lies in defining what is research and what is development. Basic research is written off as it is incurred on the grounds that it has not, by that time, produced a valuable and lasting asset and that any benefit that accrues from it is unquantifiable. No doubt the research and development staff involved in performing the work would argue with this view and suggest that it is an example of how accountants underestimate the worth of scientific and engineering effort. This sense of outrage at what is seen as a short-sighted view can be used by the creative accountant to justify the kind of accounting treatment not envisaged by the standard.

For costs to be legitimately capitalised under the standard they should relate to the construction of a fixed asset that the company will use in the business to produce saleable goods or services. The dividing line between research in its pure form and the subsequent development of profitable products or processes is a fine one indeed and the creative accountant will often be able to enlist the aid of research and development staff in claiming that as much of the expenditure as possible was used for development work.

Analysts are usually somewhat suspicious of development costs carried forward in balance sheets and many would simply ignore them in assessing the financial position of a company. This is fair enough and a legitimate part of the process of financial analysis. Few analysts, however, complete the double entry and remove from a company's earnings per share the amount of development expenditure capitalised in the year. This is important to the creative accountant since, even if he does not manage to achieve the double of boosted profits and a strengthened balance sheet, he will probably be happy to settle for the improvement to the profit and loss account.

Goodwill

Other intangible assets mentioned earlier include such items as goodwill, patents and trademarks. The question of goodwill on the acquisition of a company will be dealt with in Chapter 7. On a smaller scale, there are plenty of opportunities for the creative accountant in an expanding company to hide some of his unwelcome expenses in goodwill. The idea of goodwill is that it represents a kind of store of future super-profits above and beyond those which a particular asset or group of assets would normally be expected to produce. It occurs most frequently when one business buys another and where the real value of the acquired business lies not so much in the assets acquired but in such nebulous factors as the location of its premises vis-à-vis rivals' premises or the loyalty of its customer base.

Whenever the creative accountant is faced with the task of accounting for the purchase of a business such as this he knows that he will need to set up a goodwill item to represent the excess of the value of the whole business acquired over the valuation of the individual assets. He also knows that, in doing so, he will be able to tuck away some general expenses that the company would have incurred had the acquisition not taken place but which he can now allocate to the purchase transaction. This might include the cost of some of senior management's time or a proportion of the annual legal costs. Thus, another unwanted expense disappears from the profit and loss account to re-emerge much later, the timing to depend on the policy adopted for the amortisation of goodwill.

Patents and trademarks

Much the same can be done with patents and trademarks. Many companies need to protect their inventions, products and processes by means of registering patents and trademarks and there is usually no objection to capitalising the legitimate costs of creating these important assets. Both represent future economic benefits to their owners by allowing them to reap super-profits from the exclusive use of their inventions or by licensing them out.

What is objectionable, however, is the use made by the creative accountant of these balance sheet items to provide bolt-holes for costs that should properly be charged to the profit and loss account in the period they are incurred. It is not difficult to justify the inclusion of all sorts of overhead in these items on the grounds that the administrative set-up of the company has been provided to support all of the company's activities and that that includes the protection of the company's assets. Thus, a fair proportion of the total overhead should be charged to the creation of patents and trademarks and capitalised. Of course, the operative word here is 'fair'; it is a matter of fine judgement what is fair in this context and the creative accountant will stretch his judgement as far as he can to include the maximum amount of overhead. Many companies take the view that, since the overhead would have been incurred anyway, it is not logical to capitalise any of it. This is perhaps the only 'clean' policy — once the principle is accepted that capitalising some of the overhead is possible, then it is difficult to argue with all but the most outrageous allocations.

Provisions

When all the possibilities of deferring costs have been exhausted, the creative accountant will turn his attention to the other available opportunities for manipulating the level of expenses that go into the profit and loss account. The next item on his hit list will usually be the provisions that he has in his balance sheet for known and anticipated future expenses.

As we saw in Chapter 2, it is the Companies Act itself that provides the basis for manipulation in this area. One of the major types of provision in the accounts of most companies will be that intended to cover the permanent diminution in the value of its fixed assets. The law not only requires that, where a permanent diminution has occurred, a provision be set up, but that when it is no longer needed, it must be written back. Chapter 2 showed how this requirement could be used to manipulate the value of the fixed assets in the balance sheet, and a moment's thought will show how the other side of this accounting entry will provide scope for manipulating the profit and loss account.

When the creative accountant needs to reduce his expenses or bring some additional credits back into the profit and loss account, which amounts to the same thing, he will take a close look at the provision for permanent diminution. He will consider carefully the justification that was put up when it was originally created or when it was most recently adjusted to see whether that rationale is still valid. (Of course, it may not have been valid then, but that's another story.)

Armed with this rationale, he may now be able to argue that conditions have changed and that some of the provision is now no longer required. He is not really supposed to use inflation as an excuse here, but he will sometimes be able to do so if the value of the asset has increased due to a general increase in prices and if the original provision was based on out-of-date price levels.

This ploy can work in both directions and when the expenses seem too low and the creative accountant is looking for a way to reduce profits discreetly, he might suggest that a provision may be needed in respect of a particular asset. There can hardly be a company in the country that does not have, somewhere in its balance sheet, some assets that are not worth their stated value. The creative accountant can hide behind the traditional virtue of prudence when suggesting that a provision be made and it will not usually be too difficult to persuade the auditors that such an adjustment is necessary.

When, in the future, the same creative accountant claims unabashedly that some or all of the provision is no longer needed and that it can be written back, he is not likely to be criticised for having set it up in the first place. Better to be prudent and to be proved wrong than to have overstated the profit everyone will say, and the creative accountant will cynically bask in the approval of the profession and the public.

There are other provisions, of course, that provide scope for expense-smoothing like this. Many balance sheets will contain provisions for slow-moving or obsolete stocks, for product warranties and for bad debts. Other provisions may include amounts set aside for unfunded pension liabilities and for deferred taxes; these will be looked at in more detail later on. All of these provide plenty of scope for the creative accountant.

What should happen, of course, is that a neutral and honest assessment should be made of the situation and the appropriate adjustment made regardless of its effect on the profit. The difficulty for auditors and users of accounts is that it is virtually impossible to distinguish the cynical manipulation from the impartial, professional exercise of judgement. Even when it is possible to make this distinction, it is difficult to do much about it since it is not obvious to outsiders what the correct numbers should be. If it is a major issue, of course, the auditor may find it necessary to resign. The infrequency of auditor resignations must mean either that it does not occur often or that it is not material—or could it be that auditors just don't find out about it?

Reserve accounting

At one time, reserve accounting was a major scandal in the UK. Companies would happily charge items to their reserves and then bring them back out again without ever putting them through the profit and loss account. Such was the myopia of the City and other users of accounts that this practice went unchallenged, if not unnoticed, for many years. It was justified by its perpetrators on the grounds that the profit and loss account should only contain items that related to the accounting period in question and the normal activities of the company, and that it should not be cluttered up with items that were untypical or related to prior years. The City, they claimed, had forced them to do this due to its blinkered view of their results and by unduly penalising them for events that were one-off, outside their control, or did not relate to the period under review. While there was some merit in these assertions—the rationale of the creative accountant always contains enough of the truth to make it plausible—the proper solution was not reserve accounting.

The response of the accounting profession was to develop an accounting standard—SSAP6. This standard, which has had to be revised a couple of times to enable it to deal with abuses, is still regarded by some people as something of a voluntary standard as an examination of a selection of company reports will confirm. The basis of the standard is that the profit and loss account should contain all the profits and gains and expenses and losses that have occurred in the year. This has not stopped the creative accountant, particularly since some reserve accounting is still allowed by other standards.

Extraordinary or exceptional?

More important, perhaps, for the creative accountant with both eyes on the City is the distinction between extraordinary and exceptional items. Outside the arcane lexicography of the accounting profession these two terms might be considered to be synonymous but to an accountant there is a world of difference. This difference relates to the calculation of the earnings per share figure that features in the all-important P/E ratio. Simply put, earnings per share excludes extraordinary items but includes exceptional ones. There is, therefore, a considerable incentive for the creative accountant to classify costs as extraordinary rather than as exceptional. Then, regardless of the look of the profit and loss account as a whole, the earnings per share figure can continue its inexorable upward climb.

The difference between extraordinary and exceptional items is reasonably easy to define but is very difficult to enforce effectively. The most recent revision to SSAP 6 strives manfully to tighten up the definitions but seems doomed to failure in the face of opposition from the creative accounting community. Extraordinary items are intended to be only those events outside the ordinary business of the company, such as its complete withdrawal from a business sector or an extraneous event such as the expropriation of a major portion of its business or the effect of a natural disaster.

Exceptional items, on the other hand, are those which any company can expect from time to time but which may not occur very often or are particularly material in one year. These would include the rationalisation costs resulting from plant closures and the reorganisation of the business. Companies are expected to take such occurrences on the chin as being part of the rich tapestry of commercial life and the normal process of adjusting to the changing economic environment.

As may be obvious, the dividing line between exceptional and extraordinary is a fine one indeed and the standard cannot hope to provide guidance which will cover every eventuality. It does, however, contain a considerable amount of guidance which is intended to explain and amplify its requirements but it would have to be the size of the *Encyclopaedia Britannica* to be able to stamp out all the possible abuses. In many cases in practice, the creative accountant and his equally persuasive board of directors will be able to justify whatever treatment is their preferred choice and the reported earnings per share figure will reflect this.

Some companies, it is true, have begun to publish earnings per share figures after extraordinary items as supplementary information and this is very welcome. It also explains why the P/E ratio for a company is different in different newspapers. Those practising creative accounting in this area, however, are hardly likely to draw attention to it and, even if they were to do so, there is some doubt about whether the financial analysts and other commentators would pay enough attention to it. What they and the financial press want is one number that they can rely on—the *Financial Times* is not likely to publish a whole array of P/E ratios for each company depending on which definition is used. It is this enthusiasm for the single number that is supposed to tell all about a company that gives the creative accountant his opportunity. If he knows that the other disclosures in the accounts will not be regarded as important, he will ensure that he applies his massaging skills to those that are.

Changes in accounting policy and prior year items

Quite apart from the extraordinary/exceptional debate, the creative accountant can find scope in changes in accounting policy and prior year items. Under SSAP 6, these are still allowed to be charged directly to the reserves and avoid the profit and loss account altogether. The distinction between changes in accounting policy and changes in the estimates on which so much of conventional accounting is based is another of the grey areas which readers of this book will have come to recognise as the raw material of accounting creativity.

For example, in the area of accounting for deferred tax and the calculation of depreciation, the charge for the period is heavily dependent on the assumptions made. Whether these assumptions change the whole basis of accounting for these items or whether they are merely part of the ongoing process of tacking toward the right answer is a moot point. The creative accountant will want to keep this distinction as vague as possible so that he retains the maximum flexibility to put the effects of a change in accounting estimate, which should go through the profit and loss account, straight to reserves on the back of a so-called change in accounting policy.

Accounting policy changes will often have a double advantage for the creative accountant. The initial reason for the change may well be the desire to avoid what are seen to be the unfortunate consequences of a current accounting policy, and the opportunity to put the whole retrospective adjustment straight to reserves without hurting current profits may be an additional benefit.

A somewhat blatant case was that of Tenneco, an American oil company. Tenneco had traditionally used the less conservative of the two permitted methods of accounting for its oil exploration costs. This method, known as the 'full cost' method, allows even unsuccessful exploration expenditure to be capitalised in the balance sheet so long as the company's other oil and gas assets at least cover the full capitalised cost of the successful and unsuccessful wells.

The sudden and dramatic fall in the oil price in 1985 and 1986 meant that Tenneco faced an enormous write-off of its oil assets which had to be put through the profit and loss account. In the nick of time, it changed its accounting policies from full cost to the more prudent 'successful efforts' method and was thereby able to put the whole of the write-off directly to reserves on the grounds that it reflected the effects of the accounting policy change. Even though its shareholders' funds dropped rather alarmingly, its earnings per share actually increased and would have given a rather one-sided picture to anyone who did not take a look at the balance sheet.

While this is an extreme example which received a lot of publicity, much the same thing could happen in the UK and if it did not relate to something as well known as the oil price collapse, it could go largely unnoticed and unremarked. The saving grace, perhaps, is that the Companies Act requires an analysis to be provided of movements on reserves and this will allow those readers of the accounts who care enough to see something of what is going on. However, alongside the glamour of the profit and loss account and increasing earnings per share, the analysis of movements on reserves does seem rather technical and dull. It is just this distaste for the backroom numbers on the part of many users of accounts that gives the creative accountant the space he needs to practise his dubious art.

Chapter 7
Mergers and Takeovers

IN THE UK, the mid-1980s saw a boom in mergers and take-overs that was probably unprecedented in scale, complexity and its propensity to produce financial scandals. Quite apart from the Guinness-Distillers take-over, which has probably become the latest example of what Edward Heath called 'the unacceptable face of capitalism', the prolonged spate of merger mania has been particularly bitterly fought. In the process, it has exposed much in the area of business and financial ethics to be well below the standard formerly thought to be that of a typical City gentleman.

In any arena where the general level of business and professional ethics is somewhat shaky, one can usually be sure that the creative accountant is waiting in the wings, ready to be called on to massage, manipulate and obscure the true facts from the prying eyes of the public. There are two main reasons for using the services of the creative accountant in the context of take-overs and mergers. The first is to enable both sets of managements—that of the pursuing company and that of the pursued—to present their cases for and against the take-over in the best possible light. That usually means showing *them* in the best possible light. And nothing looks as objective and rational as the numbers produced by an accountant—or so you might have thought.

The second area that provides scope for creative accounting in the take-over arena concerns the financial reporting of the combined entity after the deal has been consummated. The arguments for the successful take-over are usually financial—or at least expressed in financial terms—and it is important for the successful management to be able to show that the promises they made and the forecasts they presented are delivered after the event. This is, of course, particularly important for the company that is frequently on the acquisition trail—the professional corporate raider—since such a company needs to establish a record of success in order to convince the shareholders of future victims that they are more likely to produce fatter profits and fatter dividend cheques than the current management. And when it comes to producing profits, who is more adept than the management team that has the use of the questionable skills of the creative accountant?

How mergers and take-overs differ

Before we look at the creative accounting opportunities in take-over situations, let us be quite clear what take-overs and mergers are and what the differences are between them. The words seem to be somewhat interchangeable, at least in the way they are used by the press, but there are significant differences. A take-over is not merely the purchase by a company of an asset or a group of assets or even of a whole business. This kind of transaction happens all the time and, although it may seem like a take-over to the people working inside the business that is sold, this is not the kind of deal which makes the merchant bankers rich. Nor is it the stuff of which City scandals are made.

A take-over occurs when one company buys another. Companies are owned by their shareholders and run by boards of directors. Except in family companies, the shareholders will not usually be the same people as the directors. What is more, even though the directors have a statutory duty to safeguard and promote the best interests of the shareholders, the interests of the directors and the shareholders will not necessarily coincide. Sometimes they will be in direct conflict. For example, the shareholders are interested in increasing their wealth and their dividend income and if they do not get the results they want from a particular company, they are free to sell their shares and invest their capital elsewhere. The directors, on the other hand, are interested in keeping their jobs, paying themselves larger salaries and providing themselves with the perks and the social status that go with the position of company director.

For much of the time, of course, these interests may well coincide, since a prosperous company will be able to provide all these benefits for its senior management and the shareholders will be happy to do so as long as the profits are rolling in. When a take-over looms, however, the interests of the directors can diverge sharply from those of the shareholders, particularly where the company is the subject of unwelcome overtures from another company. Then the directors become fearful for their jobs and their perks which they may not be able to replace easily, if at all, particularly if the take-over shows them up as inefficient and complacent. The creative accountant can then count on being drafted in by the board to help fend off the intruder.

Mergers, unlike take-overs, are much less likely to be contested and will typically involve two or more companies agreeing to merge or combine their businesses. One of the companies may well be considerably larger than the other, of course, but even when this is the case, the result of a merger will not usually be that one company is swallowed up by another as is usual with take-overs. Sometimes, a totally new entity is formed to operate the businesses of the combining entities. The original companies may set up jointly owned companies to run the combined business. One of the largest and most famous mergers occurred in 1907 when the 'Shell' Transport and Trading Company Ltd and the Royal Dutch Petroleum Company combined to form the Royal Dutch/Shell Group. Even today, both of the parent companies retain their separate, corporate identities and operate their jointly owned group together.

Take-overs, then, provide the backdrop for the first kind of creative accounting mentioned earlier. In essence any predator company's message is the same. It is that the management of the offeree company have not been as efficient, smart or even as lucky as they might have been in maximising the profitability of their company or the price of its shares on the stock market. We, say the management of the offeror company, could have done better and would do better. If only the shareholders in the offeree company would sell us their shares or—even better—exchange them for some of ours, they would become wealthier and happier. It is, therefore, an argument about who is the better manager and brings into play questions of capability, competence and integrity. And any argument that brings these issues into play can very quickly develop into a war.

In a successful take-over—successful from the point of view of the offeror, that is—the outcome is that one set of shareholders sell out to another and the acquired company forms part of the group headed up by the offeror. The acquired company becomes subservient to the other, to be expanded, contracted, sold on or wound up at the discretion of its new owner.

The most usual outcome of a merger is that the combined businesses continue. From an accounting point of view, the difference between a merger and a take-over is that in a merger no resources leave the group. After a merger, the resulting entity will be the sum of the prior entities. Put another way, when one company is taken over by another a sale and an acquisition take place. And, as we shall see later, this distinction between an acquisition and a merger is crucial to the subsequent accounting treatment and is the key to the creative accounting opportunities in respect of the resulting entity.

Mergers are less likely to give rise to creative accounting as a means of justifying the proposed arrangements unless, of course, one of the parties is deliberately trying to fool the other into accepting less generous terms than are justified by the facts. Or perhaps both are trying to convince their own shareholders to agree to the merger, remembering that each board of directors may have its own undisclosed reasons for preferring it, in which case creative accounting could have a part to play.

Preparing for action

Pre-acquisition creative accounting is usually concerned with the manipulation of previously published figures or, as it is sometimes put, the 'reinterpretation of the facts'. The long-term creative accountant will, of course, have had the possibilities of take-overs in mind all along in determining the accounting policies and methods to be used, particularly as regards the opportunities for changing them at the appropriate moment. As noted earlier, sudden and clearly opportunistic changes of accounting policies will often provoke criticism from the City and the financial press but both are sometimes strangely forgiving and have short memories. If suitable changes of accounting policy are put in place ahead of time, the creative accountant may be able to put his company in a position to benefit from them when take-overs come about.

Predator companies will usually, therefore, have ensured that their published record is a good one before they are ready to strike. The main elements of a good record are steadily increasing sales, earnings per share, dividends and the other indicators of good financial health and sound, dynamic management. Sometimes, the recent past contains the odd hiccup or two, so it is important to choose the right period of years when displaying this information.

As far as presenting its own record is concerned, the predator does not have to follow any particular rules and can produce whatever numbers it likes.

The numbers it publishes will normally be those that have previously appeared in its published financial statements. This is clearly intended to demonstrate that these numbers are not open to doubt, although as we have already seen, such confidence may be misplaced. The following example shows how previously published information can be re-presented in a way that completely changes the message it gives. Let us consider a hypothetical company whose actual earnings per share over a ten-year period have been:

77	78	79	80	81	82	83	84	85	86
20p	25p	40p	15p	30p	20p	30p	50p	75p	100p

Thus, over the ten-year period the increase has been from 20p per share to 100p per share, a fourfold increase. Not too bad, you might think, representing an annual increase of approaching 20 per cent. After allowing for inflation, of course, this is not quite as marvellous as it first seems but it is not bad.

What do not look so good, however, are the two sudden falls in earnings per share in 1980 and 1982. There might be good reasons for these falls, of course, such as substantial investments in those years which gave rise to exceptional costs and higher depreciation before the benefits of the investment began to come through into the profit and loss account. But the conventional wisdom is that the City and other commentators do not like profits bouncing around all over the place—especially if the analysts failed to forecast the changes! So the creative accountant looks around for opportunities to remove these blemishes from the record and, if possible, make the picture look even rosier. He will doubtless spot that a better picture emerges if he takes only a five-year view:

82	83	84	85	86
20p	30p	50p	75p	100p

This trend not only eliminates the unfortunate decreases in profits in 1980 and 1982 but now shows a fourfold increase in just five years—a much higher annual rate of increase.

The creative accountant on the defending side, assuming he has access to all the figures, would no doubt respond by drawing attention to the 1979-1982 trend which showed a decline of 50 per cent and would argue that the recent surge in profits could well be followed by another setback. Perhaps the profits had come from acquisitions and could not easily be repeated. If so, he would draw the conclusion that the 1979-1982 period was one when the predator management was reduced actually to running a business instead of boosting its profits in the short term by buying other businesses on the cheap. Creative accountants are not particularly inhibited about drawing attention to the creativity of others while continuing to massage and manipulate for all they are worth.

The opportunities for this kind of manoeuvre are endless and there have been many examples in recent history. One of the most notorious cases was the Distillers take-over when the newspapers were filled day after day with different interpretations of the relative records of Guinness and Argyll Foods—each by courtesy of the other's merchant banks and creative accountants. By the end of the campaign no one quite knew what the real picture was, which was the point of the exercise, no doubt.

Accounting after a take-over

The pre-acquisition possibilities for creative accounting are nothing compared with the performance that goes on after the take-over has been consummated. Then it is especially important for the management of the acquiring company to be able to show that all the promised benefits have been achieved—particularly as some of the new shareholders will be former shareholders in the acquired company and anxious to see whether or not they made the right move in selling out when they did.

The starting point is to ensure that the base from which the new trends will be measured is as flattering as possible. The first ploy, then, will be to examine the accounts of the newly acquired company to see what can be written off. This may seem a strange thing to do, having just spent a small fortune—or perhaps a large one—in buying the company, but it has a number of advantages.

The first of these is that it puts the former management firmly in the wrong. The need to make a substantial write-off, justified on the grounds that many of the acquired company's assets are obsolete and that there are unrecorded liabilities and losses, reinforces the claim made during the take-over battle that the previous management was not to be trusted with the running of the company. It also allows the incoming management to tut-tut and imply that the situation was even worse than had been feared and to suggest to the previous shareholders that they had been rescued in the nick of time.

The message goes on to suggest that there is no need to despair, however, since the business is now in the hands of more competent management. The clearing out of the corporate Augean stables was necessary so that the business can have a new start under new management. Not only can the write-off be blamed on the previous management but the subsequent dramatic improvement can be attributed to the new. Much of the improvement is inevitable, of course, since the write-off will have reduced the carrying value of many of the assets and the future profit and loss accounts will, therefore, be spared the burden of a considerable amount of depreciation and amortisation charges.

In any event, the new loss base will make any later improvement seem more dramatic than it really is. And what is more, the acquiring group will not necessarily have to take the write-off on the chin if it can reasonably claim that it is an extraordinary item. Even when it is not extraordinary it may well be exceptional so that its mere disclosure may persuade some analysts to ignore it in assessing the company and the performance of its management. It seems an amazing trick—buying something for good money, then saying that it was not worth what was paid for it and finally turning it into a star performer! In a perfect world, this kind of sleight of hand would not work, of course, but in the demi-monde of creative accounting such events are commonplace.

Goodwill

Having cleared the ground, the creative accountant now turns his attention to the thorny problem of goodwill. Goodwill is one of those ephemeral things, an intangible asset. It would perhaps not exist at all were it not for the insistence of accountants that if you have paid good money for something it must exist. (This is not consistent with the premise for the write-offs mentioned above, but by now the reader will have abandoned any hope he may have had of expecting consistency in the world of creative accounting.) In simple terms, goodwill is the difference between the fair value of the assets acquired when a company is taken over and what has been given in exchange for them. It only arises on a take-over and not on a merger since generally accepted accounting principles insist that a take-over is an acquisition whereas a merger is, well, just a merger. The point about an acquisition is that the consideration given must be valued at its fair value and not just its current book value in the accounts of the acquirer. The reason for this rule, now enshrined in SSAPs 22 and 23, is that the opportunity cost of the acquisition is clear to the shareholders of the acquiring company.

Suppose, for example, a company that wishes to take over another company offers its own shares in exchange for the shares of the company it wishes to acquire. Its own shares may have a nominal value of only a few pence but this amount has no real meaning other than being the amount that was originally subscribed many years ago. Today the value on the stock market might be £10 or more for each share and it is this value that should be used in recording the cost of any asset purchased by the issue of new shares. This is the amount that the company could have raised had it issued the shares in the market and used the proceeds to buy the target company.

The difficulty with this rule for some companies is that the assets acquired as a result of purchasing another company could be considerably less than the fair value of the shares issued or the cash paid. The difference is goodwill and the treatment of this item in accounts has been controversial for many years. It is a controversy that has not really abated with the publication of SSAP 22 which, although intended to deal with this subject, is so full of loopholes that it does not really standardise practice at all.

SSAP 22 says that goodwill should either be written off directly to reserves, written off immediately to the profit and loss account, or amortised over its useful economic life. Thus all the possibilities are allowed and the creative accountant can take his pick. The problem with a direct write-off to reserves is that, although it avoids sullying the profit and loss account with a nasty debit, it does require that adequate reserves exist in the first place. Direct write-offs to the profit and loss account or amortisation are not popular with boards of directors since this burdens the future with just the sort of charges that will make the claims to have improved upon the performance of the previous management more difficult to sustain. The amazing increase in profitability that is the stock-in-trade of the creative accountant is more difficult to produce. The reader will not be surprised to discover that there are ways round these problems.

When the acquiring company's reserves are not adequate to cover a direct write-off to reserves, the solution is to create some more. This is by no means as impossible as it sounds and it has been done in a number of well-publicised cases—and probably in many more less well-known. One source of additional reserves is provided by the simple expedient of revaluing properties and other fixed assets. The additional reserve is the difference between the revalued amount of the asset and its previous carrying value or, to put it another way, the unrealised profit due to the increase in value of the asset. If the asset is freehold land or another asset that does not need to be depreciated, then the company does not even have to suffer any additional future depreciation on the increased book value. Even where the asset does have to be depreciated, a little judicious juggling with the useful economic life will often make this a reasonable price to pay.

There is considerable uncertainty about to which of the reserves goodwill is to be charged and, while it seems clear that the standard intended that distributable reserves should be used, it does not actually say so. Some companies have successfully used the share premium account in spite of the law-makers' clear intention that this is not a suitable use for it. The share premium account is usually considered to be an extension of the share capital account and to comprise a part of the permanent capital of the company. Charging goodwill to it is tantamount to reducing that capital which may not normally be done without the permission of the court.

Some companies have gone even further than this and have ignored the fact that their reserves were inadequate and have written goodwill off against them nevertheless. The result in mechanical bookkeeping terms is that the reserves then show a debit balance, ie a deficit. This is clearly contrary to the intention of SSAP 22 although it is not specifically prohibited by it. Such a situation would normally be taken to mean that a company had lost a part of its share capital—a situation that would cause some alarm. Such, however, is the power of creative accounting, particularly in such esoteric areas as take-overs and mergers, that this kind of situation can pass off without so much as a murmur.

The companies that do not want to write goodwill off to reserves are required then to take it through the profit and loss account, either in one lump sum or over its useful life. Almost none takes the whole cost against profit at one go. Some guidelines are provided for determining what the useful economic life of goodwill is, but these are not mandatory and are widely disregarded by the creative accounting fraternity. Periods of up to 40 years are common for this purpose even though it is practically inconceivable that such an elusive asset as goodwill could retain its value for even a fraction of that time. In short, a creative accounting opportunity is exploited to the full with the result that the amortisation charge in the profit and loss account is minimal—again, clearly contrary to the intention of the standard.

The amount calculated for goodwill itself is, of course, not the result of a scientific and inviolate computation but is dependent upon creative accountancy, personal judgement and expert opinion. Placing a fair value on the assets acquired is fairly difficult even when it is done honestly, but when it is undertaken with the required end result firmly in mind it is extremely difficult to challenge. Moreover, the allocation of the amount between assets that depreciate and those that do not is an important consideration for the creative accountant. If he is anxious to avoid depreciation in the future, he will seek to allocate as much as possible of the total value to freehold land. It will, of course, be necessary to provide some kind of independent valuation to support this allocation, but the value of land can vary considerably depending on the assumptions that are made about its use and, in practice, a wide variety of valuations may be available. Thus, if the so-called fair value is capable of being massaged, the value attributable to goodwill may even disappear altogether.

The goodwill figure may not arise at all if the combination can be made to conform to the accounting requirements of a merger rather than an acquisition. SSAP 23 allows that if a combination qualifies for merger accounting then fair values do not enter into it and the accounts of the merged group are simply the sum of the pre-merger accounts of the merging entities. They are presented as though they had always been merged and this treatment has a number of advantages.

Not only is there no goodwill to be dealt with either through reserves or through the profit and loss account, but the assets acquired (sorry—merged) will be valued in the merged accounts at their current carrying values and no fair value assessment has to be made. This means that the accounts of the merged entity can continue to charge depreciation on the pre-merger carrying values which will almost certainly be lower than current fair value and will mean a lower depreciation charge than would have been required under acquisition accounting. Merger accounting is, therefore, a firm favourite of the creative accountant.

Merger accounting

There is one snag about merger accounting: a merger is supposed to have occurred. Not an unreasonable assumption, one might think. The problem with this, however, is that the acquiring company may not wish to merge with the acquired company, it may wish to take it over. This may also be wanted by the shareholders in the target company who may not want to exchange their shares for shares in a merged entity but may be more interested in taking the money and running, especially if they bought the shares in the expectation of a bid in the first place.

SSAP 23 requires that, for merger accounting to be allowed, at least 90 per cent of the consideration for the purchase of shares must be by way of shares in the offeror company. Where this condition is not fulfilled, acquisition accounting must be used with all its problems of goodwill and higher depreciation—a double penalty in the eyes of the creative accountant. So does this really mean that merger accounting is not available when the selling shareholders want money rather than shares? In theory, yes, but in practice, not at all, thanks to the ingenuity of the creative accountant and his colleagues, the creative merchant banker.

The way round the requirements of the accounting standard is a scheme known as a 'vendor placing' or a version known as 'vendor rights'. A vendor placing, usually arranged by the merchant banker or a stockbroker, works as follows. The acquiring company proposes a share exchange deal with the shareholders of the target company under which no cash changes hands. Thus, the conditions for merger accounting are satisfied and the acquiring company is free to practise it in respect of its new subsidiary. The merchant bank or broker then arranges to sell or 'place' the shares issued by the acquiring company, on behalf of the shareholders of the target company, to a group of institutional investors. The price that will be paid for these shares is agreed in advance and the proceeds are paid directly to the shareholders in the target company. Thus, the selling shareholders get their cash, the acquiring company gets to use merger accounting and the merchant bankers and the stockbrokers get their handsome fees. Everyone is satisfied except, of course, the accounting standards setters, whose intentions have been thwarted. In practice, therefore, the standard can easily be avoided by those who can afford the fees, even though the letter of its requirements is complied with perfectly.

Vendor rights is much the same type of ploy, except that the newly issued shares are purchased by the acquiring company's existing shareholders in proportion to their current holdings. This then looks very much like a normal rights issue, except that, instead of the proceeds of the issue going to the issuing company, they go to the shareholders of the target company. Of course, had the acquiring company actually had a rights issue and used the money to buy the shares in the target company, it would have had to use the dreaded acquisition accounting. So, as the old song says, it ain't what you do, it's the way that you do it, that's what gets results.

Chapter 8
Tax

MANY FINANCIAL ADVISERS used to have a saying that 'paying tax is better than not paying tax' by which they meant that only people with incomes or companies with profits paid tax. Since paying tax was an unavoidable corollary of having income, it was therefore an indicator of wealth. Such sayings are not heard much today, particularly in the boardrooms of major companies where tax would seem to be regarded as a voluntary contribution to the country's finances which could largely be avoided if one applied a little effort and some planning.

Tax avoidance

The tax avoidance industry has, in recent years, become a major feature of business life and employs a considerable proportion of business talent. Few companies can afford an overly relaxed attitude to the minimisation of its tax liability and most will take great pains to ensure that maximum advantage is taken of all the reliefs and allowances available. Many of the best brains in the business world line up daily to do battle with the best brains in government service in the never-ending, intellectual tug-of-war that is the process of agreeing tax liabilities. Any sign of weakness on the part of one side is immediately pounced on by the other in the continuous game of spot the loophole and plug it.

As an activity based on using the letter of the rules to extract the maximum financial advantage, creative accounting has much in common with the tactics used by tax avoidance experts. These include the careful use of timing, creating legal form to obscure economic substance, and misrepresenting the true nature of transactions.

Just as corporate tax avoidance provides many opportunities for the reduction of the tax bill due to the vast complexities of the legislation and case law, so does the corporate tax charge provide plenty of scope for the creative accountant. The tax charge in the accounts is much less certain than an individual's tax bill due to the interaction of foreign taxes, different UK taxes and the fact that much of the corporate tax bill can effectively be deferred for many years. This is complicated by the fact that many large organisations which have complicated tax affairs — and that means most of them — will not finalise their tax returns for as long as ten years after the end of the accounting period to which they relate since the negotiations with the UK and foreign tax authorities can go on indefinitely.

The basic principle that underlies the relevant UK standard — SSAP 15 — is that the tax charge in the accounts should represent the amount of tax that will eventually have to be paid — never mind when — on the accounting profits shown in the profit and loss account. The main difficulty of complying with this is that the tax is calculated not on the profit and loss account version of the profit but on another version which can be completely different.

It is partly because the Inland Revenue is aware of the enormous scope that conventional accounting provides for creative accounting that it has arranged for Parliament to provide it with an alternative set of rules for determining the amount of taxable profit and how much tax should be paid on it. For example, no matter how much or how little depreciation a company provides in respect of its fixed assets, the amount of fiscal depreciation — known in the UK as capital allowances — that it can deduct in arriving at taxable profit is fixed by the tax laws. Furthermore, capital allowances are based only on original cost so no amount of judicious revaluation of fixed assets can affect the amount that is claimable.

Generally, only actual costs are allowable so that the jiggery-pokery engaged in by creative accountants in creating provisions and then releasing them are of no avail in influencing the tax bill. This does not mean, however, that creative accounting is not a force to be reckoned with in calculating the reported tax charge, nor that a company can do nothing to affect its tax bill. In many cases, creative accounting will have a major role to play in determining what the final payment to the Inland Revenue will be.

The effect of this can be seen from a close inspection of the tax items in the accounts of many major companies. Although the nominal rate of corporation tax is now 35 per cent, the tax charge in the accounts may be considerably different from 35 per cent of reported profit, even over the long term. An examination of the source and use of funds statement will also show that the actual tax payments made in the current and previous years were quite different again. Often, very little additional useful information will be provided about the nature of the tax charge and its composition in spite of—or perhaps because of—the generally accepted view that a clear understanding of the tax-paying position of a company is essential to a proper appreciation of its financial position and prospects.

The variation between the nominal rate of tax and the actual rate on the one hand, and the tax payments made on the other, is due principally to two types of difference between the financial accounts and the tax accounts. These are known as timing differences and permanent differences.

Timing differences

Timing differences occur when items of income or expense occur in different periods in the financial accounts and the tax accounts. The most important of these relates to depreciation. As mentioned earlier, the tax man will not allow the depreciation charged in the financial accounts to be used for tax purposes. The capital allowances that are allowed instead may not reflect the same depreciation rate or the same method as those used in the financial accounts. Thus, while the total amount allowed over the full period of ownership of the asset will be the same for financial depreciation as for capital allowances, the timing will be different.

Typically, the rate of depreciation implicit in capital allowances has been greater than the financial rate and at one time capital allowances in the UK were 100 per cent which meant that the entire capital cost could be deducted from taxable profits in the year of purchase. In the financial accounts the corresponding depreciation would be written off over several years. Now that capital allowances have been reduced perhaps the most important difference is that they are calculated on a reducing balance basis whereas most financial depreciation is calculated on a straight-line basis.

The creative accounting opportunities associated with timing differences relate to the requirement in SSAP 15 that deferred tax—

the tax on the timing differences—should be provided to the extent that a liability is expected to crystallise but should *not* be provided if the tax is not expected to crystallise. Since all timing differences must reverse at some time in the future, whether this reversal results in the crystallisation of a tax liability will depend on whether the timing differences are replaced with new originating differences. This will, in turn, depend on whether further capital expenditure will be incurred in the future since it is only by incurring such expenditure that new originating differences can come about.

Clearly, the question as to whether future capital expenditure will occur in the amounts and in the right years to create new originating differences is a matter of judgement. Where matters of judgement exist, creative accounting opportunities exist. The standard says that it expects reasonable assumptions to be made and envisages that these will be supported by plans, budgets and other evidence. In the best run companies, such evidence will usually be available and will form part of the normal process of management. It is not difficult to see, however, how such plans could be massaged and directed towards producing the desired result. Certain versions, characterised as being 'more realistic' or—better still—more prudent, could be advanced in support of a particular view of what the deferred tax charge should be.

Since the deferred tax charge affects the current year's profit which is available for distribution and therefore the number that goes into the earnings per share calculation, it is an ideal candidate for the creative accounting treatment. What makes it even more useful is that any manipulation of the deferred tax charge does not have any cash flow impact since the amount will not be paid to the Inland Revenue for many years, if at all. It can be used, therefore, to stow away profits in good years and to release them in leaner years in the classic profit-smoothing manner.

If the objective is to raise the charge and thereby reduce the after-tax profit, it is necessary to prove that some of the timing differences will reverse in years when no originating difference will occur or when such differences will be inadequate to prevent liabilities crystallising. This is usually done simply by adjusting the timing of planned future capital expenditure without necessarily changing the total amount. Such an adjustment can be characterised as a prudent view, which is much loved by auditors, and to which the shareholder will not be expected to take exception.

If, however, the creative accountant needs to reduce the charge, he will have to show that few if any liabilities will crystallise and that, as the timing differences reverse, they will be taken up by new originating differences on new capital expenditure. When a company has a reasonably good record in forecasting capital expenditure, it should be able to sustain this argument for many years, even when that record begins to falter. Paradoxically, if and when capital expenditure does fall short of the forecast in one year, the creative accountant will often be able to argue that, far from having to reduce the following year's forecast, it will be necessary to increase the rate of capital expenditure to catch up with the investment programme.

Timing differences can, of course, operate both ways. In the UK, timing differences have usually concerned amounts that are claimable in the tax accounts before they are reflected in the financial accounts, thus giving rise to a deferred tax liability. There are many instances, however, where an expense is charged in the accounts before it is allowable in the tax return. On the basis that the additional tax paid will be offset by a future tax deduction, these timing differences give rise to deferred tax assets.

Conventional financial accounting, based strongly on the need for prudence, does not always feel the same way about assets as it does about liabilities. It requires that, while all known and expected losses and liabilities should be provided for, only those assets that are virtually certain to be collected should be taken into the accounts. This applies as much to tax assets as to other sorts of asset and it is this lack of symmetry that provides many of the opportunities for manipulation that are seized upon so gratefully by the creative accountant. In practice, it is possible to hide these tax assets by being somewhat tentative about their recoverability until they are needed for the accounts, at which time the creative accountant suddenly becomes much more certain about their recoverability and much more assertive in expressing this view.

Permanent differences

The accounting treatment of permanent differences also provides opportunities for presentational manipulation. Permanent differences arise when items of income are not taxable or when items of expense are not deductible in calculating taxable profits. One example of this arises in connection with foreign currency gains and losses. These are considered by the tax man to be capital items and not part of income. Thus, neither exchange gains nor exchange losses form part of the taxable profit even though they may appear in the financial profit and loss account. There seem to be rather more non-allowable losses than there are non-taxable gains, but both provide plenty of scope for creative accounting.

When faced with a permanent difference the accountant has to decide whether to recognise the additional tax payable or the tax relief immediately in the accounts or whether this difference should somehow be amortised over a number of accounting periods. The honest accountant will decide this issue, as all others, on the basis of the facts of the case and taking into account the true economic substance of the transaction giving rise to the permanent difference. The creative accountant, on the other hand, will decide what he wants the answer to be and will then put his argument together and his evidence in place.

In the case, for example, of a gain or loss on the repurchase of a company's own debentures, it may be possible to argue that the whole tax effect should fall in the year of repurchase. This tax effect will be that this part of the company's profit will not bear a tax charge since the profit is considered a capital one and is not subject to tax. On the other hand, it could be argued that the profit really relates to the remaining period of the loan and should be apportioned to the accounting periods on a pro rata basis. If the creative accountant is keen to reduce the apparent tax charge in the current year, he will use the first argument to take the whole benefit at once. If, however, he sees that he will need some help with the tax charge in future accounting periods, he will adopt the second argument and defer some of the benefits until later.

A similar situation occurs in the oil industry in connection with Petroleum Revenue Tax. Some of the oil produced in each accounting period is free of Petroleum Revenue Tax but no carry forward is allowed into future periods. Some oil companies take this relief when it occurs while others regard it as a relief that relates to the whole oilfield over its full productive life and spread the reduction over many accounting periods. The different treatment may be due to a genuine difference in accounting philosophy, but one suspects that the driving force is, sometimes at least, what the accountant thinks that profit and loss account can afford that year.

Creative accounting and tax minimisation

It is, of course, quite legitimate for a company to do everything that it can within the law to minimise its tax burden. There is an old saying that 'there is no equity in a tax statute' which means that the rules may be interpreted literally and that if they do not say that tax has to be paid, then the intention of the law-makers does not have to be taken into account. The strategy adopted by companies when negotiating their tax liabilities with the Inland Revenue will sometimes hinge on a particular accounting treatment even though, as mentioned earlier the calculation of taxable profit is done, for the most part, using the taxmen's own rules.

There will be times, however, when the normal rules of accounting will be regarded as persuasive as to whether, for example, an item is taxable revenue or non-taxable capital. Under such circumstances, even the most honest and straightforward accountant may find himself coming under pressure to go along with a rather dubious accounting treatment if it is thought that by presenting an item in a particular way a favourable tax treatment might be obtained or that it would otherwise support a particular tax planning strategy.

For example, a company might be claiming to the Inland Revenue that a particular item in its profit and loss account was 'wholly and exclusively' incurred for the purpose of the business, thus entitling the company to deduct it in its tax accounts. The amount may be large and negotiations on the nature of the item may go on for some considerable time. The preparation of the accounts cannot usually await the outcome of these negotiations. The accountant and the directors will have to make a judgement about this item in finalising the accounts—if it is an allowable expense the tax charge can be reduced accordingly but if it is disallowed the tax charge will be correspondingly higher.

The accountant's dilemma is obvious. If, on the grounds of prudence, he assumes that the amount will not be allowable and provides for tax at the higher amount, the Inland Revenue and its advisers could seize on this accounting treatment as evidence that the company itself does not believe its claim that the amount is deductible. Thus, the accountant may be prevailed upon to prepare the accounts on the basis that the item is deductible even if he thinks that the chances of obtaining the tax relief are small. This shows how the honest accountant can easily be drawn into creative accounting and that the distinction between honest accounting and fudge and massage is a fine one.

Advanced Corporation Tax (ACT) also provides opportunities for profit manipulation and the creation of hidden pots from which future earnings can be supplemented when necessary. ACT is paid by a company when it pays dividends to its shareholders and can be used by the company to offset its 'mainstream' tax liability. Many companies have been so effective in reducing their mainstream corporation tax liability that the ACT they pay exceeds their mainstream liability. While they can carry forward ACT payments to offset against mainstream liabilities indefinitely, they can only keep these payments in the balance sheet as long as there is a reasonable chance that they can be used to reduce a future tax bill. Where the chances of a company paying mainstream tax in the future seem remote, the relevant accounting standard—SSAP 8—requires that ACT be written off as part of the tax charge.

Thus, a company that wishes to retain this item in the balance sheet will have to show that it expects to have to pay mainstream tax in the future and this will involve, once again, forecasts and plans about the business, its future profitability and the effect of these upon its tax position. As noted in connection with accounting for timing differences, the need for judgement in the preparation and presentation of these plans provides countless opportunities for the creative accountant. When profits can stand the extra tax charge, the creative accountant produces plans and forecasts that show that the company will not be able to use its ACT carry forwards and will write them off. This provides a nice little cushion for the bad times when the picture can be reversed and the ACT, which had previously been written off and, therefore, no longer appeared in the accounts, could be used to reduce the tax charge magically.

This ploy may be easy to spot if the auditors insist on some disclosure, which they might if the amount is material. The creative accountant may, nevertheless, be able to avoid too much publicity regarding this item since the tax notes to the accounts are read only by the enthusiastic few, being regarded by most readers of the accounts as too difficult by half.

At least one company has been able to flout SSAP 8 without apparent difficulty and in a way that kept ACT out of the profit figure altogether. The argument put forward was that, since the ACT charge was brought about by the act of declaring a dividend rather than by the process of producing taxable income, then the ACT charge represented a part of the cost of the dividend. It was, therefore, according to this argument, not a charge to the profit and loss account at all, but a distribution of profit. Thus, the profit after tax and the earnings per share figures did not reflect this payment to the Inland Revenue.

The permutations seem endless and the complications of tax accounting are such that the lay reader of the accounts with only a rudimentary understanding of tax matters cannot hope to understand what is going on. The accounting policies note in the accounts should help in unravelling this mystery but, in practice, few companies seem willing or able to do more than the bare minimum in explaining the tax charge in their accounts. This is unfortunate since, for many companies, it will be one of the more significant items.

Accounting for deferred tax seems to rely more heavily than most areas on the integrity and neutrality of the accountant and the sharpness of the auditor's eye. This may be asking too much of the accounting profession at the present time, given the enormous pressures on companies to produce the profits that the City wants from them. Current accounting standards on this topic may be too permissive, or at least be seen to be so by the authorities, and there is a significant risk that if the profession cannot regulate itself, a future government may lose patience and step in.

Chapter 9
Foreign Currencies

THESE DAYS A company does not have to be ICI or Unilever to have a major portion of its operations outside the United Kingdom. Most companies of any size undertake transactions that are denominated in foreign currencies and many that would not consider themselves multinational have foreign-based operations of one sort or another. These vary in size and significance from a single sales agent in Bolivia to a major production and marketing subsidiary in the USA whose profitability might be crucial to the economic well-being of its parent.

Transaction exposure

There are two problems with foreign currency accounting: transaction exposure and translation exposure. The results of foreign currency denominated transactions will have to be expressed in sterling in the company's accounts since its shareholders will expect to be told about the company's profits and financial position in the same currency that they originally invested in it. For many companies a transaction in a foreign currency may be a one-off deal or a temporary phase in its operations. Whether the foreign currency transaction represents an isolated incident or a regular feature of its trade, the accounting problem associated with it is one of transaction exposure. This means that the company runs the risk that, during the course of the transaction, the exchange rate will change from that which prevailed at the outset and so the result in sterling will be different from expected. This could result in either a gain or a loss compared with the originally expected result and, more alarmingly, it could mean that a transaction that was profitable at one exchange rate will show a loss at a different one.

113

For example, a company may contract to sell a product to a US customer for $100,000 at a time when the dollar-sterling exchange rate was $1.25 to the pound and when the costs of completing the contract were £70,000. The profit expected on the contract would be £10,000. If, after the costs have been incurred but before the proceeds have been received, the exchange rate changed to $1.50, the proceeds of the contract would be worth only £66,667 and not £80,000 as planned and, as a result, the planned profit of £10,000 turns into an actual loss of £3333. Such large changes in exchange rates used to be rare but are now much more common and a daily movement of 2 or 3 cents no longer produces much comment.

The creative accountant and his ally, the creative treasurer, do not like to see this sort of fluctuation. Even windfall profits may be regarded as something of a mixed blessing if they cause profitability to become too volatile. The City will not take them seriously but will react like sulky children when they don't happen in the following year. The creative accountant does not like to leave matters to chance in this way and prefers the rolling downs of the massaged profit and loss account to the excitement of the roller-coaster.

The solution to the problem of transaction exposure owes more to creative financial management than to creative accounting perhaps, but the motive is much the same—the desire to avoid significant gyrations in the reported profit. Two possibilities are usually explored: invoicing in sterling or taking forward exchange cover against the currency risk. Both have the same net effect, that of effectively fixing the exchange rate in advance, but each does so by transferring the exchange rate risk to different parties.

Invoicing in sterling is not usually popular with the customer since it means that he has to bear the exchange rate risk. He may, of course, make a profit if his currency strengthens against sterling but he will probably be reluctant to take the downside risk even if it is small. If he is forced to do so, he will usually require that the price he is paying for the goods or services reflect that risk and be lower than it otherwise would.

By *taking forward cover*, the supplying company effectively contracts, usually with a bank, to sell the foreign currency proceeds at some time in the future at a rate which is agreed now. The forward rate quoted by the bank will enable the creative accountant to 'lock in' to that rate and ensure that any future change in the rate does not affect the profitability of the contract. Thus, the bank takes over the exchange rate risk which it may be happy to do because it may have another customer who wants to take out forward cover in the opposite direction.

Taking forward cover does mean, however, that the company gives up the opportunity to make an exchange gain on top of the trading profit on the transaction; if the exchange rate is more favourable at the time of payment than it was at the time the forward cover was taken out, the profit accrues to the bank. It should be noted that the forward rate quoted by the bank is not a forecast of what the spot rate is expected to be at the future date, but is determined mechanically by the difference in the interest rates available in the two currencies.

Once a transaction has been invoiced in sterling or forward cover has been taken out, no further transaction exposure remains and it will be accounted for in sterling as though no foreign currency was involved. But what if no cover has been arranged, the invoice is rendered in the foreign currency and the exchange rate moves during the period so that the company is exposed to the risk? What creative accounting opportunities are available to the lucky or luckless company?

As so often in creative accounting, the answer depends on whether the result is a profit or a loss. For example, the cynic will say that losses are always extraordinary and that profits are always exceptional. In the case of transaction profits and losses it is also a matter of where they show up in the profit and loss account—and, therefore, whether they are in or out of the important ratios.

Some accountants would always put transaction profits and losses in the profit and loss account proper under a caption such as 'interest expense and other financial charges' if losses, or a corresponding income account if profits. There does seem to be a choice, however, and it may pay the creative accountant to include them in revenue since this could have an advantageous effect on the gross margin. The truly creative accountant will probably find some way of putting some in revenue and some in interest income or expense, depending on the required result. And you can be sure that he will have a plausible reason for whatever approach he chooses and why it does not amount to inconsistent accounting.

Translation exposure

More complicated accounting problems arise in connection with the second issue in dealing with the effects of foreign currencies—translation exposure. This reflects the need to prepare consolidated accounts in a single currency—usually that of the parent company—even though the reporting currencies of the subsidiary companies are different from this currency and from each other. The principal question to be decided is simple—at what rate should the accounts of the foreign subsidiaries be translated for the purposes of consolidation? The answer is by no means simple and, even though the issue would seem to have been settled in accounting standards terms, there are many who disagree with the prescribed solution. There are others, of course, who don't care much either way but are happy to use the confusion to doctor the accounts.

The issue among the purists boils down to two schools of thought: those who believe in the temporal method and those who believe in the closing rate-net investment method. Advocates of the temporal method, under which the accounts are translated at the rate that applied when the assets and liabilities in those accounts were acquired, argue that this is the only method that is compatible with the historical cost approach.

The advocates of the closing rate-net investment method, on the other hand, say that a parent company is not interested in the individual assets and liabilities of its subsidiaries but in the net investment in each of them, and will attempt, as a matter of prudent financial operations, to match the currencies of its net investments with those of the liabilities taken on to finance them. Thus, they argue, it is the net investment that should be translated, at the closing rate at the end of the accounting period, with the assets and liabilities of the subsidiary effectively netted off.

For better or worse, accounting standards setters in both the USA and the UK have decided to require the closing rate-net investment method although the USA did, at one time, have an accounting standard based on the temporal method. This standard was heavily criticised while it was in force, mostly because it required foreign currency liabilities to be translated at the closing rate—it would have used the future rate had it been knowable—and required the resulting profit or loss to be put through the profit and loss account. No corresponding adjustments were made in respect of fixed assets, even if the liability had been taken on to finance them, and these continued to be translated at the rate ruling at the time they were acquired.

The result of this standard was that reported earnings were very volatile and the effect of this was widely regarded as 'creative accounting' and at odds with economic reality. It was true that this standard was widely misunderstood by the users of accounts and the demands, largely from business, to move to the closing rate-net investment method finally proved irresistible and it became the standard accounting practice on the issue of Financial Accounting Standards Board statement 52.

So what opportunities for creative accounting are provided by the closing rate-net investment method? There are a number of them and they involve the choice of the actual rate used, the choice of functional currency to be used by subsidiaries, which currency a particular transaction is denominated in and, possibly, the choice of the parent group's reporting currency.

The main difficulty in untangling the effects of translation exposure as reported in the accounts of international companies is knowing what the numbers mean. The most difficult number to untangle is the currency translation difference shown in the group reserves. In truth, this is no more than the balancing figure which is produced when all the assets and liabilities have been translated. It is generally considered to be incapable of being explained other than in mechanical bookkeeping terms and this shortcoming provides the creative accountant with a most convenient let-out. If it cannot be explained in business or economic terms, it is hardly likely to be challenged. If it cannot be challenged, it provides a neat bolt-hole for all sorts of nasties.

This situation is potentially further confused because the UK standard—SSAP 20—allows the use of the closing rate or the average rate during the year for translating the profit and loss account, although the closing rate must be used for the balance sheet. If the average rate is used for the profit and loss account, the statement of source and use of funds will not provide the usual link between the profit and loss account and the balance sheet. This linkage can only be made under these circumstances by first adjusting the source and use of funds statement from the average rate to the closing rate. This adjustment is difficult to understand and opens the door to accounting creativity.

Which rate to use

Clearly, the first step for the creative accountant is to decide which rate he will use in the profit and loss account translation and whether and when to switch to the other. There is a respectable argument for the average rate in that the transactions reflected in the profit and loss account will have occurred throughout the year and that the average rate represents them better than the rate on the last day of the accounting year. But the creative accountant will, of course, only have one eye on the theory and the other on the result, and it cannot be coincidence that when the pound is steadily strengthening a large number of companies with significant foreign operations are seen to switch from the closing rate to the average rate. This improves what might otherwise be a not so healthy trend were it translated at the closing rate each year. It remains to be seen whether this trend operates in the other direction and this could be a useful subject for some accounting research.

Some additional fine tuning can be achieved by changing the way the average rate is calculated. The standard does not lay down how this should be done and some companies use a weighted daily rate and some a monthly average. Some restate earlier interim accounts which were originally translated at the average rate for the quarter to the average rate for the year to date. This is quite a handy trick for the creative accountant since the effect of this is that the sum of the quarters' profits is different from the full-year figure. This non-articulation provides wonderful cover for all sorts of other skulduggery so long as it is kept within reasonable bounds.

Reserve accounting revisited

Other creative accounting opportunities stem from the rules in SSAP 20 about what goes in the profit and loss account and what goes in the balancing item in reserves. The general rule in the standard is that gains and losses on foreign currency borrowings should be put through the profit and loss account regardless of whether they have actually been realised at the balance sheet date. These gains and losses, however, may be deferred if the borrowings are intended to finance foreign currency denominated assets or are a hedge against a foreign currency asset. Both of these provisions in the standard allow for a good deal of manipulation by the creative accountant.

Although the standard allows gains and losses to be put through the profit and loss account, and prudence generally requires the recognition of losses, it may be possible to keep the gains out if that is what is required. All one has to do is to express doubt about the recoverability of the amount or part of it and it will be quite acceptable to hold the gain over to a later period—when, perhaps, it is needed more. The auditors and the public will then applaud the creative accountant for being prudent and conservative. As we have seen, creative accounting is not about flying in the face of conventional wisdom, but is all about having the best of both worlds by keeping within the letter of the law and accounting standards but choosing when to adopt a particular stance.

Functional currencies of subsidiaries

Different results will emerge from the process of foreign currency translation depending on the choice of the functional currencies of the subsidiaries. The functional currency of a subsidiary will usually be the one in which it keeps its own books and which it considers to be its home currency. This may or may not be the local currency of the country in which it operates. For example, a gold trading subsidiary operating in London may regard the US dollar as its functional currency since this may be the currency in which it conducts most of its business. Equally, the marketing subsidiary of a UK company located in a country which is experiencing very high inflation may adopt sterling as its functional currency since it may not be possible to measure its performance accurately in the local currency.

Clearly, the currency in which the foreign subsidiary keeps its own books will affect how currency differences are reported in the consolidated accounts. For example, suppose a British group had a French subsidiary and a Swiss subsidiary. It decided to raise a loan in Swiss francs but was able to locate that loan either in the French or the Swiss subsidiary. If the loan were located in the French subsidiary, any gains or losses on that loan would appear in the French subsidiary's profit and loss account since it was not hedging a Swiss franc net investment, and would flow through into the consolidated profit and loss account. If, however, the loan were located in the Swiss subsidiary, any gains and losses might be regarded as hedging part or all of the Swiss franc investment and could be deferred in the consolidated accounts.

The permutations are practically endless. One can imagine a British company taking a sterling loan, putting it into a company with a foreign functional currency and reporting a difference on exchange in its consolidated accounts when sterling moved against that foreign currency. This could result in the ludicrous situation of a British company reporting a foreign currency gain or loss on a sterling loan. All that would be needed to make the situation perfect would be to obtain tax relief on any loss; unfortunately, this is unlikely as the tax man is considerably less gullible than the average reader of accounts.

Choosing the currency for a transaction

Another variation on this theme would be to denominate particular transactions between group companies in particular currencies regardless of the real currency of the transaction. For example, a British company could make a sterling loan to its American subsidiary. If the exchange rate between the dollar and sterling changed, the US subsidiary would report an exchange gain or loss, assuming the loan was a short-term one (it most certainly would be if the intention was to produce this effect) and the gain or loss would flow straight through into the consolidated profit and loss account. Another ridiculous situation, therefore, where an intra-group loan in sterling could give rise to a gain or loss in the profit and loss account of a sterling group.

The above examples illustrate graphically the opportunities that the interaction of exchange rates can have on the financial reporting of a group that operates in a number of countries and in a number of currencies. These examples are simplified and reasonably easy to follow but imagine the problem of trying to make sense of the accounts of a group operating in, say, ten currencies. These currencies would have 45 cross-rates between pairs of them, any one of which could have been used to calculate gains and losses on any number of transactions. Interpreting the resulting gains and losses would be difficult enough in the best of circumstances and assuming full disclosure. If, however, the creative accountant has been at work, the chances of understanding the real situation are probably negligible. By the time he has finished choosing currencies, choosing rates, manipulating transactions and deferring gains and losses (although not necessarily all of them), the chances are that even he no longer has any idea of what the true situation is. At which point he administers the *coup de grâce*, changes the group's reporting currency and all remaining hope is lost.

Chapter 10
Special Purpose Creative Accounting

SO FAR WE have been looking fairly exclusively at the use of creative accounting techniques and methods in published financial reports. This emphasis reflects the widespread use of company accounts for a variety of purposes and the reliance placed on them by their users. These accounts are prepared for the shareholders, but are increasingly used by other interest groups such as trades unions, customers and potential customers, suppliers, current and potential providers of loan finance, competitors and governments.

Accounts that provide information to a wide variety of users who have different interests in the financial position and performance of the company are usually known as general purpose financial statements. In addition to these, a wide range of other financial reports is prepared for the use of particular groups or for special purposes. In this chapter, we look at these special purpose financial reports and see how the creative accountant is able to use his doubtful financial skills to massage and manipulate these numbers. As with published financial reports, the creative accountant's objective is to produce the required answer or response and not merely to present a neutral and unbiased picture of the true position.

The creative accountant's strongest weapon in this never-ending process of manipulating the accounts is the belief, prevalent among non-accountants, that accounting cannot be manipulated and is merely the application of a set of well-known and immutable rules. It is perhaps not surprising that this view is widespread in relation to external financial reporting, given the existence of the legal rules and accounting standards and the legal imposition of the audit requirement. What is quite staggering, however, is that the business world in general should have the same faith in internally generated accounting numbers.

The creative accountant is, however, equally at home operating on the company's internal financial information as he is on the external accounts. The trouble is there are a lot more of them working on the internal numbers, they have different bosses, different priorities and different objectives. What is more they look and sound just like honest, straightforward accountants so it is very difficult to tell them apart.

Whatever a company's internal management accountants might tell you, the purpose of the management accounts is not to show how the company is doing. It is to tell top management how junior and middle management are doing and which of them should get the biggest rises, the biggest offices and the biggest cars. There is not a costing system, not a management reporting process or an evaluation technique that is not capable of being manipulated so as to advance the cause of particular managers and their divisions. In short, creative accounting is running amok in the internal accounting systems of many of our largest and most important companies.

Budgets

Let's begin by looking at budgets. Most companies have, by now, been convinced by the hectoring hordes of consultants and academics that they need budgetary control in order to survive. They have also been convinced that, for their budgets to be useful and to have the power to motivate managers to perform better, they must be prepared in conjunction with the managers themselves. Sometimes they are prepared by the managers alone without any input from the top echelon. These managers are not quite alone, of course, for they have their friendly creative accountants at their sides.

Managers know, of course, that they are going to be monitored on the basis of the budgets they prepare. It is not surprising, therefore, that they prepare and submit budgets that they can meet, if not with their eyes closed, at least with no great effort. The process of putting up a budget that looks good but is reasonably easy to meet constitutes the process of 'padding' and this occurs on both sides of the profit and loss account. Typically, managers put in the padding in conjunction with their divisional accountants and the managers and accountants at head office look for the padding and take it out again. The trouble is, head office don't know how much padding there is, so they might take out too little or too much. Knowing that this happens, the divisional accountant puts in a bit more padding for good luck, and so it goes on.

Padding begins with the sales figures that go into the budgeted profit and loss account. The divisional managers know that head office will be looking for a reasonable increase over the current year, assuming, of course, that the market is expanding, and they will want to show willing by offering a reasonable increase. They will not want to offer too much since their bonuses may depend on beating this target. So their first step is to understate the growth of the market and one way of doing this is to forecast an arithmetic growth rate when the market is more likely to be growing geometrically. For example, if the market has grown from 100,000 to 110,000 units in the previous year, the budget might assume that it will grow by another 10,000 units in the following year.

In reality, if the market has grown by 10 per cent in the past year it might be expected to grow by the same percentage in the following year, ie by 11,000 units. Thus, the creative accountant has used reasonable-seeming data in the wrong way in order to provide 1000 units of padding which the divisional manager can keep up his sleeve. When the market is contracting, the creative accountant will probably undergo a conversion to the geometric school of thought for obvious reasons. The same trick can be used to forecast selling prices and the combination of a little volume and a little price change up the sleeve can amount to a tidy sum kept out of the budget.

On the expenses side of the profit and loss account, the padding operates in the opposite direction, of course, since it is in the interests of the creative accountant and his manager to inflate the size of the cost budget. A number of techniques is employed here, including using only the most pessimistic assumptions, double counting and plain overstating. By assuming, for example, that inflation is incurred all at once at the beginning of the year or that all the vacancies in the division will be filled from day one, additional amounts can be justified in the budget on the grounds of prudence.

The creative budget accountant will usually appeal to the reasonableness of top management by claiming that the budget should be approved in full so that it will not be necessary to come back part way during the year for a supplementary one. Top management may even be sympathetic on the grounds that they would also rather have a conservative budget which may provide a pleasant surprise when it is beaten than an optimistic one that will be gradually eroded during the year as additional requests are made for increased budgets.

In his real, but secret, budget, the creative accountant will know that the vacancies cannot and will not be filled until well into the year and that inflationary cost increases can be resisted for some time. Thus, he will have created another little pocket of packing.

A second technique is double counting. In the published financial accounts this would amount to false accounting, but in the internal accounts there are no auditors and very few enforceable rules so the creative accountant can get away with much more dubious practice than he can with those accounts that he publishes for the outside world. There is a number of ways of double counting, but one of the most popular is to include, in the capital budget, an investment that is justified on the grounds that it will save on costs, but to include, at the same time, the higher, pre-investment level of costs in the operating budget. If spotted, which it probably won't be, the creative accountant claims either that the cost savings will not occur until the following period—when the investment will, of course, have been forgotten about—or that he needs the cover in the operating budget in case the capital expenditure is not approved or does not go ahead for some other reason.

Another double counting technique occurs when one division incurs costs that are subsequently charged to another division. The incurring division puts the costs into its budget and conveniently omits the recoveries or understates them, while the receiving division budgets for the incoming charges that it expects it will have to bear. This may occur in respect of computer charges and other services that are provided centrally. Some companies operate elaborate mechanisms whereby the totality of intra-group charges are required to net out to zero, but this will usually be very time-consuming or politically too difficult to police effectively. If it is not done, however, considerable double counting may slip in.

Plain and simple overstating of likely costs is much more difficult to spot, particularly since the skilful creative accountant will attempt to move the focus of the overstatement each year. A moving target is rather more difficult to hit than a stationary one. Ironically, some companies lay themselves open to this by basing their evaluation of one year's budget on the previous year's actuals or, where these are not available, on forecasts of what they will be. These forecasts are, of course, produced by the same managers and accountants who have prepared the budgets that are being appraised.

This process, therefore, leads to the situation whereby the more that is spent in one year, the more that is approved for that budget the following year. This tends to encourage and reward overspending and over-budgeting. This may be real or fictitious; real overspending occurs when divisions desperately spend money at the end of a year not only to justify the level of that year's budget, but also to support the case for the following year's proposal. Inevitably, much of this money will be wasted. Fictitious overspending occurs when the creative accountant puts through unnecessary accruals at the end of one year to increase the apparent amount spent in that year. This technique has a double effect: not only is the following year's allocation increased, but when the unnecessary accruals reverse in the following year the resulting credits provide yet more padding.

Considering how much padding goes into the budget, it is a wonder that the creative accountant has to worry too much about manipulating the actuals as they emerge from the accounting system. It is likely, however, that, no matter how skilful he has been at the budgeting stage, he will still need—or think that he needs—to tinker with the actual results.

Actuals

Since, for many companies, the rules about the internal management accounting system will be less comprehensive and less formal than those relating to external reporting, there is plenty of scope for creativity. Techniques here include moving costs from one budget to another, charging costs to other people's budgets and moving costs from one year to another. Since to do this the creative accountant has to tinker with the company's accounting system, he has to be careful that his manipulations do not involve the external accounts and do not infringe any of the legal or professional requirements that affect them.

It is amazing, though, how often adjustments, caused by internal creative accounting, are made to the published financial accounts after the end of the year. Since, however, management's attention will usually have moved on to the next financial year by the time the accounts are published it will only be the most out-rageous cases that will ever become an issue in the context of management accounts. The creative accountant will be able to use any differences in accounting principles between the financial and management accounts—and there will be some, even in the best-run companies—to mask any manipulation. If a reconciliation is prepared between the financial and management accounts, it will often be regarded as a boring, technical accounting matter and left to the backroom boys in the finance department.

Moving costs around

Massaging the management accounts will often consist of moving costs from budgets that are overspent, or look as though they will be by the end of the year, to those that are underspent. Frequently, there will be no internal control to prevent this and the creative accountant will have the run of the ledgers. He will probably choose to put the entries through at the busy time of the month when effective scrutiny and control is at its weakest and anyone who tries to check his adjustments may find themselves accused of slowing down the process of finalising the accounts—a heinous crime in most accounting departments.

When the accountant has some discretion about how costs are allocated to various budgets it will be the easiest task in the world to see that the charges go to those budgets that can afford them rather than the ones to which they properly relate. Capital budgets that are in danger of overrunning will mysteriously cease to incur costs or will suddenly be discovered to have been overcharged and will receive some refunds. A popular trick relates to the allocation of periodic fixed charges. In those periods when the charge is split between a large number of budgets and the amount charged to each is therefore low, the 'tight' budgets can afford a share. In months when the shares are larger because fewer budgets are to receive a share, however, only the underspending budgets receive an allocation.

Another weakness in many companies' internal controls over management accounts is one that allows one manager to charge costs to another manager's budget. This is compounded when one or more budget units do not have any one person responsible for them and such a budget can easily become the dustbin for unwanted costs from all over the organisation. When a company operates a complex network of cross-charging, whether or not proper controls have been installed, a great deal of dishonest cross-charging can go on that will never be challenged or discovered. Divisional managements may even connive at this since the underspending departments may be as unwilling to see a major variance as the overspending ones.

A variation on this theme is the massaging of genuine cross-charging arrangements. Quite often the arrangement will allow a division to cross-charge the whole of a particular cost centre to the other division based on its sole use of a facility or service. Not surprisingly, the cost centre in question may become another dustbin for any unwelcome or unexpected costs. If the receiving cost centre is also reallocated, perhaps to a large number of other cost centres, by the time the process finally comes to rest, it is practically impossible to identify the offending incorrect allocations and the incentive to do so will have been eroded by the arbitrary nature of the allocation process itself. If, in the eyes of the final recipients, these allocations are regarded as non-controllable costs, no one will want to know. As is so often the case with all sorts of creative accounting, the more complex a system is, the easier it is for the creative accountant to obscure what he is doing.

Moving costs between years

Costs can also be moved between years with even more ease than is possible in the financial accounts but using much the same techniques. Costs may mysteriously move in and out of stock, into and out of provisions, and creditors and costs may simply be held in suspense until the next period. It is quite amazing how many companies operate suspense or clearing accounts in their ledgers which are somehow outside the management accounts and which make ideal receptacles for inconvenient costs and revenues until a proper home can be found for them in later accounting periods.

Some costs or revenues that show up in the management accounts may not even be in the financial accounts at all. Some of these may be genuine adjustments or errors that come to light when the management accountants examine the detailed accounts but some are just 'balls in the air' that are juggled by the creative accountant in order to maintain the cosy picture that all is well and under control. This juggling act cannot go on for ever, of course, and cannot conceal major financial problems for long. But as a short-term manipulation method it is ideal. Again, the reconciliation process that is supposed to reveal this untoward behaviour is often delegated to junior accounting staff who have only to demonstrate that the accounts balance to satisfy their bosses.

Explaining variances

Having padded the budget and manipulated the actuals, it might be expected that all the creative accountant would have to do at the end of the year was to sit back and bask in the glory of having achieved or beaten the divisional budget, and to plan how he was going to spend his hard-earned bonus. However, in spite of all the effort he may have put into making sure that the future turns out the way he wants, there may still be variances from budget that he and his managers have to explain.

He won't need a great deal of creativity to explain the favourable ones. These, of course, are due to the superior performance of the divisional management, himself included. He will, however, be at great pains to explain these variances in a way that does not suggest that the budget was too easy. The unfavourable variances, on the other hand, are explained so it is made clear that the budget was too tight or that outside circumstances intervened in a way that made it impossible to achieve.

The usual way of dealing with these explanations is known as anecdotal or non-rigorous variance analysis. What should occur is that the difference between the actual results and the budgeted results should be analysed in detail and with complete thoroughness so that all the reasons for the variances are uncovered. These detailed variances can then be split into controllable and non-controllable. Only if this analysis is undertaken honestly can all the real reasons for the variance be discovered and proper remedial action taken.

Since, however, part of the remedial action could involve sacking the divisional management, the creative accountant is not overly interested in rigorous variance analysis. Instead he will choose anecdotal variance analysis which involves looking for excuses rather than reasons. Anecdotal analysis means picking enough plausible sounding reasons which can be made to account for the difference between the budget and the actual and presenting them as though they were the full picture. An example will illustrate how this might work. Imagine that the profit budgeted by a division was £10 million and the actual profit was £8 million. The full analysis of the reasons for the shortfall might look something like this:

		£ million
(a)	Market smaller than forecast	(0.8)
(b)	Labour inefficiencies	(0.7)
(c)	Raw material cheaper than budget	0.6
(d)	Cost of strike at supplier	(1.2)
(e)	Lower overhead allocation than budget	0.1
	Total shortfall	(2.0)

The creative management accountant will choose to ignore items (b), (c) and (e) since these either show the management in a bad light or, if favourable, do not reflect credit on the divisional management. The lower raw materials cost, for example, could have been the result of good negotiating by the group's central purchasing department. He will therefore present the shortfall as relating to items (a) and (d) which, he can claim, were outside the control of divisional management. This will give the impression that a profit of £8 million is not a bad result in the circumstances and will hide the fact that £0.7 million was lost by the inefficient use of labour and that this was compensated, somewhat fortuitously, by favourable events that were outside the control of divisional management.

All too often, this kind of analysis will be accepted at face value, either because head office knows no better or because nobody wants a row. One is tempted to believe that much of what is passed off as management reporting and variance analysis is no more than a sham, just a ritual designed to convince all the participants that they are efficient and rational businessmen who are interested in maximising profits for the shareholders. In this kind of ritualistic world, the creative management accountant presides over the proceedings like a numerate high priest.

Capital budgeting

The role of the creative accountant in capital budgeting is somewhat similar to his role in management reporting. Much of the power of his position is due to the fact that most people in the organisation have implicit faith in the truth and correctness of the numbers that he presents. No matter how shaky the assumptions on which a project appraisal is based, no matter how unlikely that the plant to be built can ever produce to capacity or the sales department can ever sell the output, just seeing the numbers on paper is enough to convince some people that it will all happen as predicted.

The very techniques of project appraisal seem to produce an aura of certainty and precision. The sensitivity analysis, the cash flow projections and the discounting back to present value all seem to make the process scientific and dispassionate. Yet the truth is that the role of the creative capital budget accountant will often be to work back from the required answer and produce a set of assumptions and parameters that are plausible and that will ensure that the project is approved.

If it were possible for those who have to approve the final capital budget proposal to look at the first draft of the project appraisal, the awful truth might be revealed. The initial stage might be the last time that best estimates and realistic assumptions feature in the process and necessarily so, in the view of the creative accountant, since it is only at this stage that it is possible to see how far the real expectation differs from the required outcome. Once this difference is known, the creative accountant can set to work to tweak the many variables in the equation until the final answer is fit to be exposed to senior management.

The first variable to be manipulated is the capital cost of the project. Since this inevitably occurs at the beginning of the project, it has a high weighting in the discounted cash flow (DCF) calculation. Thus, the project can be made to look more attractive if this estimate can be reduced. So it may be relieved of some of the contingency allowance which was put in by the project managers. The creative accountant will tell them not to worry too much about this since, once the project is well under way, a supplementary proposal can be submitted for the additional funds and the blame can be placed on something or somebody else.

Another ploy that will help the net present value (NPV) of the project is to defer some of the forecast capital expenditure into the second or subsequent years of the project. The higher discount factor applied to this figure will improve the NPV and make the project more attractive. It may not even be necessary to defer any of the income that is expected to flow from the investment and, since top management will not have seen the first draft, they will not know that this deferral has happened.

The creative capital budget accountant will turn his attention next to the operating costs contained in the capital budget proposal. He will be looking to trim these back or to rephase them to later years, which again improves the NPV. By the time the project has been completed and is running operationally, he knows that no one will look back at the original budget proposal. Even if someone does, there will be a million and one reasons why the situation has changed since then.

Lastly, he will turn his attention to the income forecasts in the proposal. If the estimate of market size or market share can be increased even slightly, the effect on the revenue can be quite dramatic and the NPV enhanced further. Advancing some of the receipts from later to earlier years can also transform the economics of the project significantly.

By the time this series of massaging exercises has been completed, the economics of the project should be looking much healthier. Since many companies use a pre-set discount rate for evaluating capital budget proposals it may not be possible to make any more adjustments to the proposal itself. The creative accountant may be able to argue, however, that the project is less risky than normal and that it would therefore be appropriate to use a lower discount rate. If project finance has been arranged, he might argue that the interest rate on the finance should be used as the discount rate for the project.

The latter argument, persuasive though it might sound, flies in the face of two of the most important tenets of capital budgeting theory. First, project appraisal and project financing are separate aspects and should not be confused; and second, the discount rate used should be the company's weighted average cost of capital and not its marginal cost of capital. Few people in the company are likely to have had any theoretical training in finance or to know much about capital budgeting—even the creative accountant may only have a rudimentary understanding of the subject—and his arguments may hold sway.

If he cannot persuade the company to reduce the rate of discount, the creative accountant may find that he obtains a more acceptable answer by making the calculation in real terms, ie by eliminating the effects of general inflation. This is achieved by using constant year 0 prices and costs for the whole of the project and a net-of-inflation discount rate. Since the inflation assumptions may have been provided by the accountant in the first place he may have more control over the answer than he has in after-inflation terms.

Transfer pricing

The creative accountant in a divisionalised company may be called upon to exercise his manipulative talents on a broader canvas than just a single division. In such a company, one of the more obvious areas for the application of his dubious skills is that of transfer pricing. This can be done for fun, for profit or both.

Some sort of transfer pricing is necessary in all divisionalised companies where cost or profit responsibility is delegated to divisional management. It may also be necessary for tax or excise duty reasons or because transactions cross corporate frontiers in a group.

The most important rule to remember in connection with transfer pricing is that there are no rules. There is no universally agreed method which is the most appropriate in all circumstances. There exists a whole spectrum of possibilities and the one that is chosen in a particular set of circumstances will be the one that will do the job it is intended to do in those circumstances. Despite the totally arbitrary nature of all transfer pricing, the chosen method will doubtless be defended with great vigour by the creative accountant as the only possible approach in the particular situation.

Transfer pricing is all about putting the costs and profits of an organisation where you want them to be. If the objective is the minimisation of the group-wide tax charge—and this is often the driving force behind much of transfer pricing—the creative accountant will aim to locate the largest taxable profits in the areas where the rate of tax is lowest. He will, of course, need to take into account any problems this might pose for the repatriation of profits to the parent.

To do this, the creative accountant will need to come up with good reasons for increasing the cost of goods and services transferred by the group into highly taxed countries and for reducing those going into tax havens. Occasionally, or perhaps often, he will construct transactions that have no real business substance at all in order to obtain the same effect. This can involve management and service fees, royalties and commissions payable on the one hand, and rebates, discounts and commissions allowed on the other, depending on the required result.

Sometimes the impact of a local income tax system and the import duty arrangements conflict and produce a double burden. When the tax rate and the import duty rate are both high the creative accountant will have to balance the two and assess the overall effect. Ideally, he would like a high transfer price for incoming goods for tax purposes and a low one for import duty purposes but this is difficult to achieve without arousing the suspicions of even the dullest-witted local officials. Often the preferred solution will be a lowish transfer price combined with a relatively high procurement and transportation commission if the latter does not attract import duty.

Another reason for the creative accountant's interest in transfer pricing may be the existence of a joint venture with a third party or the existence of a cost-plus contract. In both cases, some or all of the costs of an enterprise may effectively be borne by a third party and it is in the interests of the company that the charges to the joint venture or the contract are as high as possible. Clearly, the terms of the venture or the terms of the contract will prohibit straightforward cost-dumping, but the application of some creative accounting thought should throw up opportunities for profitable massaging.

Common techniques here include allocating the highest cost staff or equipment to the venture or contract or allocating common corporate costs on a basis that ensures that the venture or the contract gets more than its fair share. Sometimes the opportunity arises to provide company-produced goods and services to the venture or the contract at market value rather than on the basis of actual cost. If labour charges attract an overhead recovery rate, then the more labour is chargeable to the venture or contract, the more of the company's fixed overhead is paid for by somebody else. And when the arrangement calls for the recovery of cost only, the creative accountant ensures that the definition of cost that is used is the broadest possible.

Accounting numbers are used for a wide variety of purposes in commercial and industrial situations and in dealings with government departments and agencies. Hopefully, the examples provided above have offered something of an insight into how these numbers can be massaged to fool enough of the people enough of the time. The misplaced confidence that many people have in figures that are considered to be unimpeachable provides these opportunities for creative confusion.

None of these techniques is illegal and most are not even considered unethical by many businessmen and accountants. The secret of making them work is not to allow the procedures or the terms of the contract or the venture to be too specific. If they refer to conventional accounting methods or generally accepted accounting principles, the creative accountant will rub his hands with glee. For only he knows how misplaced is the outside world's confidence in the integrity of numbers produced on this basis, and that he has much more scope for massage and manipulation than the signatories to the contract could ever imagine. He knows that there is a bit more profit in the contract or the venture than was intended, due to these possibilities, which he can earn without stepping outside the letter of the agreement. At the same time, he will be anxious to maintain the fiction that accounting is a well-regulated activity that is a science rather than an art since this is a smokescreen behind which he can play his arcane tricks.

Chapter 11
The Presentation

HAVING MASSAGED THE figures in the accounts into almost unrecognisable shape, the creative accountant has not finished with them. Before he finally has to put them on show, either before the shareholders or the top management of a divisionalised company, he still has one or two more tricks to perform.

Once the books are written up at the end of the year, the accountant does not merely hand his ledgers over to the nosy investor and let him poke about in them at leisure. He summarises the contents of the books into the financial statements that were described in Chapter 1 and, in so doing, he has one last chance to massage and manipulate. The layout and content of the annual published accounts are much more regulated than they used to be since the passing of the Companies Act 1981 (now incorporated into the Companies Act 1985). This Act sets out the formats for the profit and loss account and balance sheet in considerable detail and establishes the valuation rules to be used in the presentation of the accounts. It is generally recognised, however, that these rules have had only a limited effect in creating the uniformity that they were intended to, and the fact that most published accounts look similar nowadays disguises a great deal of divergence.

Administration costs

Take, for example, the item 'Administration Costs' in one of the standardised profit and loss account formats. The intention of this disclosure seems quite obvious and quite reasonable. It is intended to provide some indication of the efficiency of an organisation by showing how much of the gross profit of a company is consumed in running its bureaucracy. But, like many other items of disclosure

135

required by the Act, there is no proper definition provided to ensure that the same disclosure by different companies means the same thing. Thus, each company has to interpret the term 'Administration Costs' its own way and it is quite clear that different companies have taken quite different views as to its meaning.

In a large group of companies, administration costs may be thought of as the total of all the costs of administration in each and every one of its subsidiaries as well as the costs of running the head office. Since only general guidance can be issued to subsidiaries in collecting this information, the reported total may well contain a variety of costs. Overall, this item is likely to be a significant component of the group profit and loss account for many companies.

The creative accountant may not like to see such a large item in the profit and loss account under this heading as it might be interpreted as meaning that the company is overly bureaucratic and inefficient or, worse still, overmanned. (This might be the correct implication, of course, but that will not influence the creative accountant's view of whether it should stay or go.) He will, perhaps, take the view that only the costs of administering the group from head office should be included under this heading and that the so-called administration costs of the subsidiaries are actually costs of sales in a group context.

An examination of the group consolidated accounts of some of the country's major companies will show that this has actually happened; if you are really lucky, the accounting policies note will tell you how the costs have been defined. Even if no guidance is given in the accounting policies note, the vastly different relative sizes of the administration items indicate that widely differing interpretations of the requirements have been made by different companies.

Intangible fixed assets

Much the same may be happening under the other captions in the profit and loss account and balance sheet but it is more difficult to spot them. For example, the distinction between tangible and intangible fixed assets is an important one in a number of respects. The Companies Act requires a separate disclosure to be made of intangible fixed assets and that this amount be deducted from reserves in calculating the amount that is available for distribution at any time. Yet many, if not most, companies happily add

into their tangible fixed asset items such intangible costs as legal
expenses, interest and overheads, and may or may not disclose
this in the accounting policies note.

Accounting policies

The whole question of accounting policies provides the creative
accountant with an enormous amount of scope. With the deft use
of changes in accounting policies, he is able to conjure up more or
less profits, more or less assets and better trends, as we have
already seen. The constant changing of accounting policies may
seem at odds with the accountancy profession's general concern
with consistency and that the accounts should be comparable from
one year to the next. So how is the creative accountant able to use
changes of accounting policy to massage the figures and trends
without running into legal or professional problems?

The answer is with care and proper preparation. Clearly, he
cannot zigzag backwards and forwards between different policies
and methods as the fancy takes him. Such cavalier treatment of
the consistency principle would certainly create problems with the
auditors and analysts. But the creative accountant can reasonably
claim that circumstances change and that the company cannot be
bound for ever by decisions it made in the past and under different
conditions. Virtuously, he will point out that he is ever alert to the
need to reconsider accounting policies and will be prepared to
change whenever it seems that a new accounting policy will provide a truer and fairer view. What he is actually on the look-out for
is something quite different—the opportunity to fool a few more of
the people for a little more of the time.

For many companies, the ideal time to change their accounting
policies is at the time of, or just before, a major share issue. This
phenomenon has been observed more than once in connection with
the government's privatisation programme, although in these
cases the change has always been justified as part of the process of
putting these organisations on to a proper commercial footing. If
such a process involves making them fully aware of the power of
creative accounting, then perhaps it is appropriate, after all.

Sometimes the change in accounting policy is accompanied by a
generous write-off of the loans owed by the company to the government, which transforms the balance sheet from one that has a
rather dilapidated look to one that seems to promise a golden future

to the lucky new shareholders. Yet, in the privatisation euphoria, no one seems inclined to ask the obvious question: if the company needed to borrow so much in the past, what is so different about its future that this level of borrowing will not be needed again.

The newly minted profit and loss account, shorn of its interest burden, may promise a new beginning, but is it a reasonable basis for forecasting how the future will look? No company, if it is being realistic about its future, would rely on free gifts along the way. In the context of the privatisation programme, the miracle of accounting policy changes and once-off generosity from the previous shareholders seems to be ever capable of fooling those who wish to be fooled. This is not to say that these companies will not prosper and serve their new shareholders well, only that their accounts represent neither the truth about their past nor a basis for predicting their future.

Accounting policy changes do not have to be as dramatic or as material as this for the creative accountant to use them effectively. A well-orchestrated programme of minor changes over the years in such mundane and boring areas as stock valuation, bad debt provisions and the recognition of profits on long-term contracts can be of more use in the long run because they are low key.

Associated companies

One particularly useful ploy concerns the inclusion or exclusion of associated companies from the consolidated accounts, particularly the consolidated profit and loss account. The accounting standard that governs associated companies is SSAP 1. This requires that, where a company owns more than 20 per cent but no more than 50 per cent of another company over which it exercises 'significant influence', it should account for that investment as an associated company using the equity method. This means that it should include, in the consolidated profit and loss account, its share of the net income of the associate and, in the consolidated balance sheet, its share of the associate's net assets.

These amounts are not actually consolidated, but are shown as a separate item. When, however, more than 50 per cent is owned, the investee company is a subsidiary and is fully consolidated. When less than 20 per cent is owned or where the 'significant influence' is doubtful, the investee should be included as a trade investment. This means that only the dividends from the investee are brought into the consolidated profit and loss account and that its profits—and, more important, losses—should be kept out.

While the intention of the standard is clear and admirable, the opportunities that it presents to the creative accountant represent a cornucopia of presentational possibilities. In the first instance, it may be possible to arrange the level of a company's shareholding in its investees more or less at will, in concert with the ever-willing creative merchant banker. For a fee, the merchant banker may buy and sell shares in the investee so that it can become a subsidiary, an associate or a trade investment at will and depending on how well it is doing.

When it is doing well, the parent may want it in the consolidated accounts as a group company and will buy enough shares to make it a subsidiary. We saw in Chapter 4 how a company could become a hidden subsidiary of another by the judicious use of differential share structures and, in this context, a company can just as easily become a technical subsidiary of another using the same sort of technique. When the investee company does less well, the parent can sell a few shares to the merchant bank and—hey presto—it becomes an associate and only the parent's share of the profit goes into the consolidated profit and loss account. The bottom line, after taking out minority interests, will be the same, of course, but this ploy keeps the associate's results out of the gross margin and brings it in again later on and further down the profit and loss account where it attracts less attention.

If the situation becomes really nasty and the investee starts to make losses, more shares are sold to the merchant banker and the offending company drops out of the consolidated profit and loss account altogether. If matters get so bad that the investing company has to write off all or part of its investment, this will probably show up but it will most likely be dealt with as an extraordinary item and, once again, the prurient gaze of the investing public and the analysts is deflected.

This sort of scheme may not be possible if the other shareholders will not play ball and, after all, they may be more interested in making money than in creative accounting. Nevertheless, some manoeuvrability still exists between presentation as an associate and as a trade investment. All the company needs to do is to change its mind about the existence of significant influence.

This is necessarily a very subjective concept and can genuinely change from time to time depending on all sorts of factors including the degree of integration that exists between the operations of the parent and those of the associate. Where, for example, the parent sells the associate a major proportion of the latter's raw materials or provides it with essential research or development assistance, this degree of integration could easily amount to significant influence. If, however, without any change in the level of shareholding, the decision is made that the associate should 'go it alone' as regards raw materials or research and development, then the requisite significant influence for equity accounting may no longer exist.

Even companies in which the parent owns more than 50 per cent may not always be regarded as subsidiaries for the purposes of consolidated accounts. There are a number of grounds advanced for the non-consolidation of subsidiaries, the most usual being that, for one reason or another, the parent has lost effective control over the subsidiary. Alternatively, non-consolidation can be justified on the grounds that the business of the subsidiary is so different from that of the parent that the consolidation of the subsidiary would produce meaningless or misleading accounts.

Both these justifications have considerable merit and many honest accountants firmly believe in them. In the hands of creative accountants, however, such reasons can be used to manipulate the accounts so as to obscure the real operations of a group and to misrepresent its financial position. Such is the concern in the USA about this problem that the Financial Accounting Standards Board has decreed that all wholly-owned subsidiaries must be consolidated unless it can be clearly shown that the parent has lost effective control. Whether the UK will follow this lead remains to be seen.

For the present, both options remain open to the British creative accountant. As far as control is concerned, once a subsidiary's profits begin to fall and if losses appear likely, the creative accountant will begin to look for evidence of loss of control. If the subsidiary is a foreign one, particularly if it is in a developing country, he will begin to wonder whether its operations are being hampered by local restrictions in respect of, for example, imports and exports, exchange control or the availability of work permits for expatriates. He will begin to collect evidence of interference in commercial policies, in pricing and in transfer pricing arrangements and in questions of quality or the terms of trade. In the end, he will probably come to the conclusion that, in spite of owning more than 50 per cent of the shares in the subsidiary, the parent has lost effective control over its operations. This conclusion is even easier to justify if the local government is also a shareholder in the subsidiary.

On the basis of this evidence, the creative accountant sadly comes to the conclusion that it would not be appropriate to consolidate the subsidiary and that its status within the group should be reconsidered. Things may have got so bad that even significant influence may no longer apply and the former subsidiary may now have to be treated as a trade investment. This may mean making a write-off of the carrying value of the former subsidiary but here, in a rare burst of optimism among the gloom, the creative accountant may see some hope for the subsidiary and convince himself and others that it need not be written off quite yet.

The really important point is that the consolidated profit and loss account should suffer as little as possible. This concern is not only for the current year where a write-off may have had to be incurred, but for the future for, if the subsidiary had stayed in and continued to make losses, these would have shown up above the line and harmed future earnings per share numbers.

If a miracle happens and the subsidiary perks up and begins to produce reasonable profits once more, then the creative accountant will have to think again. By the same process of reasoning that led him to the conclusion that it was the interference of the local government that led to the earlier reduction in profits, he will soon begin to regard the improvement in the fortunes of the subsidiary as evidence that the parent's control over it is being restored and that it can once again be regarded as determining its own operating and commercial policies free of any damaging constraints. Thus, the prodigal subsidiary will once again be welcomed into the consolidated fold, its profits will rejoin the consolidated profit and loss account, and the horrors of the past will be forgotten. What goes down might well come up again and one can be sure that the creative accountant will be alert to opportunities whatever way the wind blows at any particular moment.

Inflation accounting

While governments and pensioners may not like inflation much, the creative accountant welcomes the fall in buying power of the currency as another opportunity to massage the presentation of the figures. It is uncanny how, in times of significant inflation, company accounts are replete with five- and ten-year financial summaries, and when inflation subsides, there seems to be inadequate space in company accounts for this information.

The usefulness of a historic series of numbers like these is that the average reader of a set of accounts will not often have much of a feel for what inflation has actually been over such a long period. He may know what the inflation rate has been over the last year since this may have been reflected in a recent pay rise, and he may even remember the previous year's inflation if he has a head for figures. But he is very unlikely to know what the relative price level was ten years ago compared with today.

And so he will look at the magnificent trend in the sales figures, the profits and the earnings per share numbers without knowing too accurately what the increase should have been just to keep up with inflation. He will see that sales have doubled and that profits have increased by 50 per cent and will vote the chairman and the directors their proposed share option, not realising that this represents a fairly miserable performance and that the directors have not even been able to stand still in the face of inflation, let alone beat it by a healthy margin.

The reader will probably also turn to the other financial statistics in the glossy annual report, equally unaware that these have been rendered largely meaningless by the effects of changing prices. Such items as return on capital employed, which is made so much of by company chairmen and analysts alike, are very poor measures of the efficiency of a company, being doubly impaired by the effects of inflation.

This ratio is usually calculated by dividing the accounting profit for the year by the average capital employed during the year. Both of these figures, as we have seen, are open to significant manipulation by the creative accountant and, even without the inflationary effect, one would have to be a little suspicious of taking these figures at face value. Inflation adds two extra reasons for doubting this figure.

First, the depreciation charged in the historical cost profit and loss account is based on the original cost of the asset which may have been purchased many years ago. The depreciation charge, which is often thought of as representing the cost of using the asset, will be much lower when the asset is old than it would be on an asset that was purchased more recently. Thus, the older the fixed assets, the higher the profit after depreciation has been deducted. Second, this same low historical cost will also produce a lower capital employed figure and this distortion will be greater the older the assets are.

Consequently, a high and increasing return on capital employed in times of inflation may mean nothing more than that the assets are rather old and will probably need to be replaced in the near future. A high return on capital employed figure does not, therefore, always mean that the company is operating efficiently. When the assets are finally replaced with new, more expensive ones this ratio could drop markedly as the increased depreciation charge reduces the numerator and the higher level of capital employed increases the denominator. When this happens, it is not surprising that this particular ratio often disappears from the accounts for a while.

When prices are rising sharply, the creative accountant gets further presentational assistance in the profit and loss account in the calculation of the gross margin. Under inflation, the profits coming through the profit and loss account could also be significantly out of date due to stock bought at earlier, lower prices being matched with later, higher selling prices. In certain circumstances the selling prices could actually be lower than the cost of replacing the stock and processing it for sale. When this happens, the historical cost-based profit and loss account will be showing a profit at a time when the business cannot even be maintained at its current level of activity and is, therefore, contracting. Taken to its logical conclusion, the company will continue to report profits right up until the day it finally goes bust.

The convenient aspect of inflation from the creative accountant's viewpoint is that he does not have actually to indulge in positive manipulation to achieve the desired result. All he has to do is to let the historical cost accounting system run its course and it will do his work for him. Gradually improving profits, gradually increasing assets and gradually increasing return on capital employed statistics will all be produced automatically from the accounting system, whatever the real after-inflation position is like.

The irony of the situation is that these defects of the historical cost system are well known. Over the last ten years enormous efforts have been made by the accounting profession to develop and make operational accounting standards that would remove the distorting effects of changing prices, both inflationary ones and those relating to specific prices. At one time, the Accounting

Standards Committee had a mandatory accounting standard on the books to deal with this issue. SSAP 16 was issued in 1980, following many years of debate, but by 1986 it had died. It was complied with reasonably well at first, but as it became apparent that little attention was paid to the numbers it produced, and as general inflation abated, more and more companies began to ignore it. In 1986 it was finally withdrawn in order to preserve the ASC's credibility since it was felt that it could not allow a mandatory standard to be widely flouted.

Much of the opposition to current cost accounting, the system required by SSAP 16, came from those companies for whom the myth of increasing profitability produced by historical cost accounting was a comforting fiction which they did not want to see removed. The harsh reality, which was so often revealed by current cost accounting, was one of stagnant or falling sales, falling profitability and contracting businesses. Many boards of directors had enough difficulty facing these realities in the privacy of their boardrooms without needing to have their noses rubbed in it in public. Much of the criticism of SSAP 16 and the other attempts to deal with the effects of changing prices in accounts was based on claims that the methods proposed were too subjective and would lead to... creative accounting. Talk about the pot calling the kettle black!

Creative statistics

Creative accountants can also be creative statisticians when opportunities permit and it is noticeable how many annual reports contain charts and other statistical information that have been prepared on a rather doubtful basis. There are many excellent books on statistics and most of them deal with the abuse of statistics as well as explaining the proper application of the techniques. In this context, it will probably suffice to provide one simple example which occurs with monotonous regularity, not only in published accounts but also in the financial information published by companies during take-over battles. This is the graph with the 'suppressed zero'. This kind of chart does not have zero at the origin as it should, nor does it indicate clearly that it does. As an example, consider the following graph of sales volumes:

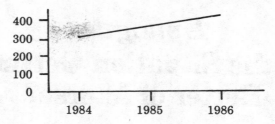

By suppressing the zero, and starting the chart at 250, the growth rate has quite a different look about it:

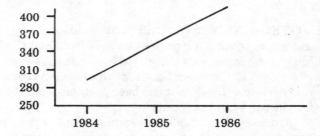

See how the slope of the graph has become much steeper? It amazes most numerate people how the rest of the world can be fooled by such crude tricks, but an examination of the debris left after a take-over battle should convince you that a lot of the people are being fooled a lot of the time by creative statistics such as these.

Epilogue
Is the Situation Getting Better or Worse?

THE FOREGOING CHAPTERS paint a rather sorry picture of the state of the accounting profession in Britain and the integrity of published financial reporting. I would not, however, like the reader to close this book without a word of encouragement. So is the picture really as black as it has been painted or are there rays of hope for the readers of accounts?

First, let me say that not all the companies in the country are fiddling their books in all the ways mentioned here all the time. There are many honest and straightforward accountants who insist on telling the truth in their accounts and whose attitude has the backing of their boards and their auditors. The real problem is, you don't know who they are. Whether the answer is that the UK should have more detailed standards and more vigorous enforcement is still an open question, but my own feeling is that this is not the way forward and would only lead to accounting standards overload and a legalistic attitude towards them. No, the right way forward is to engineer a change of attitude in those on whom the responsibility rests for setting the ethical standards to which accountants should work.

This brings me to the question at the top of this page. Is it getting better or worse? Paradoxically, it seems to be getting better and worse at the same time. It is getting better because there is a great deal more publicity given to the creative accounting debate than in the past, particularly in the financial and business press and not just in accounting journals. More and more, commentators in the press are complaining about the unreliability of financial statements that have been accounted for creatively, and the tone of the comments is becoming less and less amused. This pressure will, it is hoped, jolt many of the companies that massage their figures out of their cosy belief that they have not been spotted. Names are already being named and it will not be too long before there is a series of accounting scandals like those of the 1960s that gave rise to the Accounting Standards Committee in the first place. It is a shame that Britain always seems to need a scandal to get the ball rolling.

It is, however, the very publicity that creative accounting is getting that will probably make it worse in the short run. Some companies, whose accountants would have been creative if they had been more on the ball, have had the inner workings of creative accounting explained to them for the first time. This book may even have to share some of the blame for it. But time is running out for them and they do not have long to practise the black art of creative accounting—public opinion and professional consciences are catching up with them fast!

Appendix

Appendix

Summary of Statements of Standard Accounting Practice issued by the Accounting Standards Committee

SSAP 1: Accounting for associated companies

Associated companies are those in which the investing company exercises 'significant influence', usually by owning more than 20 per cent but not more than 50 per cent of the equity. Investing companies should bring their proportional share of the net assets and net income of associated companies into their consolidated balance sheets and profit and loss accounts.

SSAP 2: Disclosure of accounting policies

The fundamental concepts that underlie financial reporting are (a) going concern, (b) accruals, (c) consistency and (d) prudence. Companies should disclose in a note to their accounts the accounting policies that they employ in connection with the following areas: depreciation, amortisation of intangibles, stocks and work in progress, long-term contracts, deferred tax, hire purchase and instalment transactions, leasing and rental transactions, conversion of foreign currencies, repairs and renewals, consolidation policies, property development transactions and warranties for products and services.

SSAP 3: Earnings per share

This standard only applies to listed companies. Earnings per share and the basis on which it is calculated should be shown on the face of the profit and loss account. Earnings are profits after tax and minority interests and preference dividends but before extraordinary items divided by the average number of shares in issue and ranking for dividend in the period.

SSAP 4: Accounting treatment of government grants

Grants relating to fixed assets should be credited to revenue over the expected useful lives of the assets, either by reducing acquisition cost or by transferring a portion of the grant to revenue annually.

SSAP 5: Accounting for value added tax

Turnover shown in the profit and loss account should exclude value added tax.

SSAP 6: Extraordinary items and prior year adjustments

Exceptional items are defined as those of exceptional size or incidence that derive from the company's normal business and may include redundancy and reorganisation costs, fixed asset write-offs, abnormal charges for bad debts, abnormal provisions in respect of long-term contracts and insurance claims surpluses. Extraordinary items, on the other hand, do not derive from the ordinary business of the company and might include the discontinuance of a business segment, the expropriation of assets or a change in the basis of taxation.

Prior year items, which may be adjusted through reserves, are related to changes in accounting policy (not merely changes in an accounting estimate) or to the correction of fundamental errors which effectively invalidated previous financial statements. All items which are not prior year adjustments should go through the profit and loss account.

SSAP 7: Withdrawn

SSAP 8: The treatment of taxation under the imputation system

The following should be included in the taxation charge in the profit and loss account and disclosed if material:

- the amount of the UK corporation tax charge, specifying the charge on the profit for the year, tax applying to franked income, irrecoverable advanced corporation tax and overseas tax relief;
- overseas tax.

SSAP 9: Stocks and work in progress

Stocks and work in progress (wip) other than long-term wip, should be shown in the accounts at the lower of cost or net realisable value.

SSAP 10: Statements of source and use of funds

This standard applies to all companies with a turnover or gross income of more than £25,000 per annum. Statements of source and use of funds should be provided and should show, if material, dividends paid, acquisitions and disposals of fixed assets, funds raised, increase or decrease in working capital divided into its components and movements in liquid funds.

SSAP 11: Withdrawn

SSAP 12: Accounting for depreciation

Defines depreciation as the wearing out, consumption or other loss of value of a fixed asset. Depreciation should be based on the carrying value of the asset and should be charged to the profit and loss account, and no portion may be charged directly to reserves.

SSAP 13: Accounting for research and development

Basic research expenditure should be charged to income in the year that it is incurred. Development expenditure may be carried forward if there is a clearly defined project whose technical and economic feasibility have been established with reasonable certainty.

SSAP 14: Group accounts

Defines holding companies and subsidiaries. Normally, a holding company must produce a set of consolidated accounts covering itself and its subsidiaries, but subsidiaries that are very different from the parent or over whom the parent does not effectively exercise control may be excluded.

SSAP 15: Accounting for deferred tax

Distinguishes between timing differences and permanent differences between accounting profit and taxable profit. Requires that the tax payable on timing differences should be accounted for to the extent that a liability is likely to crystallise and should not be accounted for when it is probable that the liability will not crystallise. The deferred tax balance in the balance sheet should be disclosed and analysed.

SSAP 16: Withdrawn

SSAP 17: Accounting for post-balance sheet events
Events occurring after the balance sheet date may be 'adjusting' or 'non-adjusting' events. Adjusting events provide additional evidence about conditions that existed at the balance sheet date and should be taken into account in preparing the financial statements. Non-adjusting events should be accounted for in the following period.

SSAP 18: Accounting for contingencies
Material contingent losses should be accrued in the accounts where the loss can be estimated with reasonable accuracy: where these are not accrued they should be disclosed except where the possibility of loss is remote. Contingent gains should not be accrued.

SSAP 19: Accounting for investment properties
Investment properties exclude those properties owned by a company for its own use. Investment properties should be included in the balance sheet at open market value and need not be depreciated.

SSAP 20: Foreign currency translation
Requires the use of the actual exchange rate for translating the foreign currency transactions of an individual company, but closing rate/net investment method for translating the accounts of foreign subsidiaries in consolidated accounts. In the latter case, exchange differences arising on consolidations are put directly to reserves. Profit and loss accounts of subsidiaries may be translated either at the closing rate or at an average rate.

SSAP 21: Accounting for leases and hire purchase contracts
Provides rules for both lessees and lessors. The standard distinguishes between operating and finance leases and requires lessees under finance leases to account for the transaction as an asset and a liability.

SSAP 22: Accounting for goodwill

Deals only with purchased goodwill but confirms that no value should be attributed in the accounts to inherent goodwill. Goodwill may not be carried in the balance sheet indefinitely but should either be written off directly to reserves (the preferred method) or charged to profit and loss account. The charge to profit and loss account may be immediate or it may be made over the estimated useful economic life of the goodwill concerned.

SSAP 23: Accounting for acquisitions and mergers

Permits merger accounting when a business combination is primarily a share-for-share exchange for at least 90 per cent of the shares of the offeree and where the offeror held, prior to the offer, no more than 20 per cent of the equity of the offeree. A business combination that does not meet these conditions should be accounted for as an acquisition.

Under merger accounting the financial statements of the merging entities are combined without adjustment (except for intra-group items) and the resulting accounts are presented as though the merged entities had always been merged.

Acquisiton accounting requires that the consideration given by the acquirer be accounted for at its fair value. The assets and liabilities acquired should also be accounted for at fair value. An acquisition is accounted for only from the point in time that the acquisition takes place.

Further Reading from Kogan Page

Achieving Economy, Efficiency and Effectiveness in the Public Sector, Cyril R Tomkins, 1987

Finance and Accounts for Managers, Desmond Goch, 1986

The Financial Services Act 1986, 1987

Going for Growth: A Guide to Corporate Strategy, Michael K Lawson, 1987

The Practice of Successful Business Management, Kenneth Winckles, 1987

The Stoy Hayward Business Tax Guide 1987-88

A Handbook of Management Techniques, Michael Armstrong, 1986

Index

Accounting period, arbitrariness of 71
Accounting policy changes 90, 137
Accounting Standards Committee
  (ASC) 18, 66
Accruals 53
Administration costs 135
Advance corporation tax 111
Advancing payment of invoices 44
AEI-GEC 17
Allocation of fixed charges 126
Anecdotal variance analysis 128
Associated companies 138

Bad debt provision 41-3, 73-4
Balance sheet 11-13
Blind-eye approach 54
Budgets 122

Capital budgeting 129
Capital expenditure 14, 25-6
Capitalisation 83
Cash 45-50
Cash flow 48-50
Cash-to-cash cycle 71
Changes in accounting policy 90
Closing rate-net investment method
  116-17
Creative statistics 144
Cross charging 127
Current assets 12, 34-50
Current liabilities 12, 52-5

Debentures, repurchase of 109
Debtors 41-5
Deeply discounted bonds 56
Deferred expenditure 82
Deferred tax 106-8
Delaying payment of invoices 45

Depreciation methods 26-7
Detecting creative accounting 22-3
Direct labour costs 38
Discounted cash flow (DCF) 130
Discounts 35, 52
Double counting 124
Double-entry bookkeeping 13

EC seventh directive 67, 76
Equity 12
Exceptional items 89
Exchange rate, use in currency
  translation 117
Expenses 80-91
Explaining variances 128
Extractive industries 75
Extraordinary items 10, 89

Financial Accounting Standards
  Board (FASB) 56, 117, 140
Finance leases 60
Financial instruments 78
Fixed assets 11-33, 136
Foreign currencies 113-20
Freight costs 36
Full cost accounting 91
Functional currencies 119
Futures 79

Goodwill 85, 98-102
Gross margin 73

Hidden subsidiary 63-66
Historical cost convention 11

Income 69-79
Indirect labour costs 38
Inflation accounting 141

Information overload 78
Innovative financial instruments 78
Institute of Chartered Accountants
    in England and Wales 18
Intangible assets 85, 136
Interest 9

Labour costs 38
Leasing 59-61
Liabilities 12, 51-68
Limitations of accounting 15-17
Loan fees and costs 76
Long-term contracts 72
Long-term liabilities 12, 55-8

Merger accounting 102
Mergers, definition of 94
Moving costs around 126
Moving costs between years 127

Non-consolidation of subsidiaries
    63-6, 140
Non-depreciating assets 63-6, 140

Objectives of accounting 15
Off-balance sheet liabilities 58-68
Operating leases 59
Overheads 37
Overspending, real and fictitious 125

Patents and trademarks 85
Permanent (taxation) differences
    108-9
Permanent diminution in value 33, 86
Petroleum revenue tax 109
Phoney purchase schemes 61
Post-acquisition creative accounting
    97
Pre-acquisition creative accounting 95
Prepayments 45
Price/earnings (P/E) ratio 81
Prior year items 90
Production overhead 38
Profit and loss account 9-11
Property 28
Provisions 12, 86
Prudence 11
Purchase schemes, phoney 61

Reducing balance depreciation 26, 106
Research and development 84
Reserve accounting 88, 118
Reserves 13, 99, 100
Retained earnings 13

Return on capital employed 142
Revaluation 29
Revenue or capital? 77
Rules for accountancy practice 17-19

Sales figures in budgets 123
Seventh directive of the EC 67, 76
Share capital 12
Shareholders' funds 12
Significant influence 139
Source and use of funds statement
    14-15
Split depreciation 30
SSAP 1   138, 151
SSAP 2   22, 37, 151
SSAP 6   88-90, 152
SSAP 8   111, 152
SSAP 9   39, 153
SSAP 10 48, 153
SSAP 12 26, 31, 153
SSAP 13 84, 153
SSAP 15 105, 153
SSAP 16 144
SSAP 20 117, 154
SSAP 21 60, 154
SSAP 22 99, 155
SSAP 23 99, 101, 102, 155
Standards avoidance 20
Statements of Standard Accounting
    Practice (SSAPs) 18, 151-5; *and see
    individual SSAPs*
Stock purchase schemes 61
Stocks 34-41
Straight-line depreciation 26, 106
Substance over form 56, 66
Successful efforts accounting 91

Takeovers, definition of 93
Tax 10, 104-12
Tax avoidance 104, 110-12
Temporal method 116
Tenneco 91
Timing differences 106-8
Timing of delivery of goods 53
Timing of payments and receipts 46,
    53
Transaction exposure 113-15
Transfer pricing 132
Translation exposure 115-17
Turnover 9

Unit-of-production depreciation 26

Variances 128

Vendor placing 102
Vendor rights 103
Volume effects on stock valuation 40

Warehousing costs 37

Window dressing 47, 62
Working capital 14
Work in progress 34, 62, 82

Zero coupon bonds 56